$3.95
TWOJK

THE WORLD OF JEROME KERN
A Biography
by David Ewen

The year was 1905, the name of the show was *The Earl and the Girl*, the hit tune was "How'd You Like to Spoon With Me?" and it started an unknown young songwriter named Jerome Kern on the road to success. Forty years and 1,000 songs later, at the time of his death, Jerome Kern was already a legend in Tin Pan Alley.

Now the fantastic life story of this gentle little "music man" is told for the first time in a full-scale biography. David Ewen has painted a masterful portrait of Kern—the warm and ebullient human being, the creative genius whose melodies transformed America's taste in popular music.

Here is Kern the composer as seen through the eyes of his celebrated collaborators: Otto Harbach, Guy Bolton, Oscar Hammerstein II; as the creator of the memorable songs: "Who?", "Look for the Silver Lining," "Smoke Gets in Your Eyes," and the one that had the composers themselves swooning—"Ol' Man River." Here, too, are the stories behind the great musicals of a

(Continued on back flap)

.75

WITHDRAWN
No longer the property of the
Boston Public Library.
Sale of this material benefits the Library.

Boston Public Library

Purchased with State Funds

THE WORLD OF JEROME KERN

OTHER BOOKS BY THE SAME AUTHOR:

Complete Book of the American Musical Theater

Richard Rodgers

A Journey to Greatness: The Life and Music
of George Gershwin

The Encyclopedia of the Opera

A Panorama of American Popular Music

The Home Book of Musical Knowledge

*Milton Cross' Encyclopedia of Great Composers
and Their Music* (with Milton Cross)

The Complete Book of 20th Century Music

Music for the Millions

Dictators of the Baton

Music Comes to America

From Bach to Stravinsky

The Encyclopedia of Concert Music

Mr. Ewen is also the author of the following titles in
the Holt Musical Biographical Series for Young People:

The Story of Irving Berlin

The Story of Jerome Kern

The Story of George Gershwin

Haydn: A Good Life

Tales from the Vienna Woods: The Story of Johann Strauss

The Story of Arturo Toscanini

THE WORLD OF
Jerome Kern

A BIOGRAPHY

BY

David Ewen

ILLUSTRATED WITH PHOTOGRAPHS

HENRY HOLT AND COMPANY
NEW YORK

*To Bob,
the song is you.*

"Here were warmth, enchantment, laughter, music. It was Anodyne. It was Lethe. It was Escape. It was the Theater."
—Edna Ferber

Acknowledgment

Wherever possible, I went for my biographical material to first-hand sources. On each of three visits to Beverly Hills I had several sessions with Kern's widow (Mrs. George Byron) and Kern's daughter (Mrs. Jack Cummings); during my third visit they read the first draft of my manuscript and once again contributed valuable information together with advice and criticism.

Many others have also been highly co-operative in supplying me with documents, letters, clippings, programs, reminiscences, and so forth. Among those to whom I would like particularly to express my indebtedness are: Guy Bolton; Arthur Freed; Ira Gershwin; Oscar Hammerstein II; Otto Harbach; André Kostelanetz; Kern's business manager, William Kron; Kern's cousins, Walter and Elsie Pollak; Kern's New York attorney, Howard Reinheimer; Richard Rodgers; P. G. Wodehouse; and Kern's boyhood friend, Maurice Wolff.

The roster of those contacted by mail, telephone, or wire

for specific bits of information or for substantiating facts is much too long to list here; but such help cannot pass without an expression of gratitude. Gratitude must also be expressed for various favors: to Mrs. Byron, Mrs. Cummings, Walter Pollak, Lynn Farnol, Ira Gershwin, P. G. Wodehouse, Guy Bolton for valuable photographs; to Arnold Shaw of Edward B. Marks Music Corporation for a copy of Kern's first published piece, "At the Casino"; to the Drama Room of the New York Public Library for the availability of its remarkable collection of newspaper clippings and programs.

Permission to quote copyrighted material was granted by Simon and Schuster for several passages from *The Jerome Kern Song Book* edited by Oscar Hammerstein II, *Lyrics* by Oscar Hammerstein II, and *Bring On the Girls* by P. G. Wodehouse and Guy Bolton; by Doubleday & Company and Edna Ferber for several lines from Miss Ferber's autobiography, *A Peculiar Treasure;* and by Theatre Arts Books for a quotation from Cecil Smith's *Musical Comedy in America*, copyright 1950 by Cecil Smith.

—D. E.

Little Neck, New York

Contents

1. "Who Is This Jerome Kern?" . . .   1
2. A Man of Many Faces   11
3. "Romie"   23
4. From Tin Pan Alley to Shubert Alley   31
5. Eva   42
6. Victor Herbert's Mantle   50
7. "The Opening Chorus of an Epoch"   54
8. Grand Seigneur of Bronxville   66
9. Betty   72
10. Interval Between Two Epochs   75
11. "Warmth, Enchantment, Laughter, Music"   85
12. A Footnote on *Show Boat*   97
13. End of an Epoch   102
14. Hollywood   115
15. Life at Fifty   119

Contents

16. New Horizons 125
17. Grand Seigneur of Beverly Hills 132
18. "When He Goes Away, Dat's a Rainy Day" ... 139

Appendixes

I. Broadway Stage Productions 147
II. Selected Broadway Productions with Interpolated Kern Songs 156
III. Scores for Motion Pictures 162
IV. Instrumental Music 165
V. Kern's Greatest Songs 166
VI. Selected Recordings 168
Index 173

THE WORLD OF JEROME KERN

1

"Who Is This Jerome Kern?"...

In a uniquely productive career in the American musical theater that spanned the years from 1904 to 1945, Kern wrote the music for 104 stage and screen productions. Many of these productions were run of the mill; but others helped change the destiny of the musical stage. For these 104 productions he created over one thousand songs. Some are stereotypes. Many never became popular, and still represent *terra incognita* even for Kern connoisseurs, but they represent a world of melodic grace and charm whose exploration could prove most rewarding.* Almost a hundred of these songs are classics, whose survival in the living repertory of American music seems assured; and no less than fifteen are among the greatest commercial successes ever realized either on Broadway or in Tin Pan Alley.

Perhaps as good a way as any to measure Kern's stature

---

* A listing of unknown or completely forgotten Kern songs, which in the opinion of the author are well worth reviving, will be found at the end of Appendix V. See also "Première Performance" in Appendix VI.

as a composer is to use the yardstick of his influence on two other giants of the contemporary musical theater and American popular music.

One was George Gershwin. Gershwin, at sixteen, was already a serious piano student and a passionate enthusiast of American popular music when he attended his aunt's wedding at the Grand Central Hotel in New York. The band struck up two songs that made him stop in his tracks. As he listened, the songs represented to him a new world of music. Here was a radical departure in style, mood, and idiom from anything then being circulated as popular music. Gershwin rushed to the bandstand to uncover the identity of both the songs and their composer. The songs were "They Didn't Believe Me" and "You're Here and I'm Here." And the composer was Jerome Kern—a name Gershwin was now hearing for the first time.

From then on, and until he achieved his own creative identity, Gershwin used Kern as a model and an inspiration. He himself put it this way: "I followed Kern's work and studied each song he composed. I paid him the tribute of frank imitation, and many things I wrote at this period sounded as though Kern had written them himself."

The other giant early influenced by Kern was Richard Rodgers. He was also a mere youngster when Kern's music was first impressed upon his consciousness. As an avid theatergoer from his childhood on, Rodgers had been an admirer of Victor Herbert and other American composers of European-type operettas then crowding the American stage when, in 1916, he saw Kern's *Very Good, Eddie*. He himself described as "shattering" the impact that show made upon him, and has confessed that he went to see it a dozen times. He lost all interest in operettas, even those by Victor Herbert, as he sought out musicals as authentically American in book and score as some of the Jerome Kern productions were.

"The influence of the hero on such a hero-worshiper is not easy to calculate, but it was a deep and lasting one," says Rodgers. "His less successful musical comedies were no less important to a listener of thirteen or fourteen. A large part of one winter most of my allowance was spent for a seat in the balcony listening to *Love o' Mike*." Rodgers might have added that, like young Gershwin, he soon started writing songs in Kern's style.

Gershwin and Rodgers openly acknowledged their indebtedness to Kern; so have other important popular composers, including Arthur Schwartz and Harold Arlen. Several composers may be more reticent about making such a confession. But whoever has produced songs in Tin Pan Alley or labored within the musical theater in the past half-century has inescapably profited from Kern.

Kern published his first piece of music as far back as 1902; contributed his first songs to an American stage production in 1904; and achieved his first song hit in 1905. In 1905 Irving Berlin was singing other people's ballads in the saloons of the Bowery; his first published song, only a lyric at that, was still about two years off. In 1905 Richard Rodgers was three, Vincent Youmans was seven, George Gershwin, seven, and Cole Porter twelve. In 1905 the most successful Broadway composer was Victor Herbert, whose heart and pen flowed over with some of the most lovable melodies heard on our stage. But Herbert's style was more European than American, and his music was heard in plays closely patterned after European operettas. In 1905 the two big musical productions on Broadway were both foreign-styled operettas: Raymond Hubbell's *Fantana* and Victor Herbert's *Mlle. Modiste*. The big song hits of that year were

Egbert Van Alstyne's "In the Shade of the Old Apple Tree," Paul Dresser's "My Gal Sal," George M. Cohan's "Mary's a Grand Old Name," Harry von Tilzer's "Wait 'Til the Sun Shines, Nellie," and Ernest R. Ball's "Will You Love Me In December as You Do in May?" (the last to lyrics by James J. Walker then state senator, and many years later New York's dapper mayor). All these ballads had sentimental appeal and charm; but none revolutionized the accepted styles and procedures in Tin Pan Alley.

It is by placing Kern's music and Kern's musical comedies in focus with the times and settings in which he worked that impelled Arthur Schwartz to describe Kern as "the daddy of the modern musical comedy"; that inspired Irving Kolodin, the distinguished music critic of the *Saturday Review*, to say that "it might well be possible to argue that Kern invented the modern show tune as we know it"; that convinced Richard Rodgers that "the first man to break with European traditions in the theater was Jerome Kern."

When Kern produced his first important musical-comedy scores in the 1910's his concept of the role of music in a stage play was iconoclastic, since unlike most of his colleagues he was less concerned with the individual song hit and more with the score as a whole. Even then he was always searching for the proper piece of show business with which to give relevance to a song within a play. Men whose job is words and who have worked with Kern—Otto Harbach, Guy Bolton, P. G. Wodehouse, and Oscar Hammerstein II among others—are unqualified in their appreciation of and praise for Kern's sound theater instincts and his command of stage techniques.

To many other prominent composers of Broadway musicals in the 1900's and 1910's the song was always the thing;

everything else in a production had to make room for the solid hit. "They paid almost no attention to plot," reveals Otto Harbach about several composers, including Karl Hoschna and Rudolf Friml, with whom he had worked before collaborating with Kern. "They were indifferent to characters, even to the situations in which their songs were involved. They didn't even care much about the kind of lyric that was being written for their melodies, just as long as the words fit the tune." But Kern was ever most fastidious not only about lyric but also about the demands of good theater. "He knew a great deal about the stage, and what went into the making of sound theater," Harbach goes on to say. "He always looked for the 'gimmick' to make a song logical within a play, and was delighted when a song had good motivation. He also had an astute critical sense for good dialogue and plot development, and never hesitated to impress his opinions on his collaborators."

"It was characteristic," recalls Oscar Hammerstein II, "that he didn't go to the piano the first day we met. He didn't think a score is important unless it is linked to a good libretto. He was always more intense about story and characterization than about music."

So great was Kern's concern with the stage that not even the slightest detail of a production failed to escape his eye. Hammerstein recalls a rehearsal in which everything on the stage seemed to go beserk at once—not only with the actors, but even with lighting and scenery. But what upset Kern most at that very moment—and sent him screaming down the aisle—was the fact that he had suddenly noticed that the property man had forgotten to put a rubber mat under a brass cuspidor in a remote corner of the set. "I was surprised at first," Hammerstein writes in the preface to *Lyrics*, "to find him deeply concerned about details which I thought did not matter much when there were so many important problems to solve in connection with writing and producing a play. He proved to me, eventually, that while people may not take any particular notice of any one small effect, the over-all result of such finickiness like his produces a polish which an audience appreciates."

Because of his keen sense of stage values Kern could help create in the 1910's the Princess Theater Shows which were so successful in injecting freshness, informality, charm, and gaiety into the American musical, thereby bringing to existence a new genre of the theater, one intrinsically American. It was also because of his strong appreciation for sound stage values that in the 1920's he was endowed with the vision to see in Edna Ferber's novel *Show Boat,* material for a new kind of production, able to emancipate the American musical theater from its bondage to hackneyed ritual.

So desperately did Kern need the stimulation of a play, character, situation, or some bit of show business for the writing of a song, that only once in his career did he write one not originally planned for a stage or screen play ("The Last Time I Saw Paris"). All the rest of his more than one thousand numbers were meant to be part of some stage or screen production. "I am just a musical clothier," Kern once explained lightly. "I can only write music to fit a given situation, character, or lyric within a play or motion picture the way a good tailor fits a garment to a mannequin."

Those Kern songs, even as early as the 1910's, were fresh, new, daring sounds both for Broadway and Tin Pan Alley. "Who is this Jerome Kern whose music towers in an Eiffel way above the average primitive hurdy-gurdy accompaniment of the present-day musical comedy?" Thus inquired Alan Dale in 1904 upon seeing *Mr. Wix of Wickham,* in which Kern made his first appearance as a Broadway composer. In the succeeding dozen years Dale's question would be asked again and again by many others. Songs like "Babes in the Wood," "Nodding Roses," "You're Here and I'm Here," and "They Didn't Believe Me" introduced to the American popular musical idiom of the 1910's a lightness of touch, intriguing modulations, seductive lyricism, freshness of sentiment, and a sureness of song structure. Those early Jerome Kern songs are so unmistakably Kern, so characteristic of his later mature approaches that the composer's lifelong friend, publisher and business associate Max Dreyfus, was once tempted to believe that through the years Kern's style never really changed.

It is not easy to point precisely to those qualities endowing a Kern song with its striking individuality. In a Gershwin song one can single out certain ingenious uses of rhythm and meter unique to the composer; a personal way of fashioning a melodic line. We can recognize a Cole Porter song usually by its sensual climactic surges and by the background of an irresistible throbbing rhythm. In Richard Rodgers the songs are characterized by peculiarities of intervallic structure, by the narrative quality of many of the lyric lines, by the expansiveness of the song structure.

But with Kern the personal creative procedures are not so easily identifiable. Several of his best songs are in a simple 2/4, 3/4, or 4/4 time. The structure of his refrain* is often in thirty-two measures, and just as frequently falls into a formal A-B-A-B or A-A-B-A pattern of the ballad (the A and B representing different eight-bar melodic phrases). No difference here, then, from methods employed by Tin

---

* Kern himself preferred the rather rare term "burden" or "burthen" to "refrain." Nevertheless, in the *Jerome Kern Song Book* "refrain" and not "burden" or "burthen" is used consistently.

Pan Alley hacks! "His creations are bound by the same forms which govern other songs," Arthur Schwartz has written, "and they appeal to the same sentiments. Yet they aren't Tin Pan Alley at all. In them is a deep intrinsic feeling. About them is no hint of the contrived, no taint of the manufactured."

What then is Kern's secret? It is perhaps the secret of all true genius, that which separates inspiration from skillful contrivance. Within the circumscribed boundaries Kern had so often set for himself, he was able to pour a wealth of the most winning sentiment and the most poignant beauty through a lyricism that never lacked either spontaneity or originality. He always manages to do something fresh in his melodies to maintain interest, and does it so gracefully and easily that the melody falls naturally on the ear. Sometimes he achieves a climax through an octave ascent in the recall of the main melody, or through the interpolation of an unexpected minor ninth interval; sometimes he brings a novel chromatic sequence within a diatonic frame; sometimes he avoids the repetition of his main melodic thought; and sometimes he makes effective use of changes in intervallic sequences. But however he may digress from the norm in his melodic writing, the melody itself always stays fluid and graceful; it is always lovely to listen to. For—make no mistake about it!—the man who wrote "All the Things You Are," "Smoke Gets in Your Eyes," "Ol' Man River," "Look for the Silver Lining," and "The Way You Look Tonight" is one of America's supreme melodists.

One reason for Kern's seemingly inexhaustible lyric invention within the circumscribed limits of the four-measure phrase, the eight-bar line, and the thirty-two measure refrain was his fastidious craftsmanship. He was painstaking to seek out an ever more graceful turn of phrase, a surprising inflection, a more effective transition, or a fresh thought. Simplicity and directness came to Kern only after the most extensive revision and refinement. When he was through, there was about his songs almost the same feeling of inevitability we encounter in Schubert.

The beautiful symmetry, balance, and directness of his writing has made his music the easiest in the world for which to write lyrics. Otto Harbach says: "His music was so simple in its construction and in its conversation-like rhythm that adapting words to it proved an elementary chore. A lyric like 'Smoke Gets in Your Eyes' took me no time at all, so easily did the melodic flow adapt itself to the words."

Though Kern wrote a considerable amount of functional pieces for specific purposes and performers, and though he always maintained he was writing not for posterity but merely for the pleasure of his contemporaries, he had a severe artistic integrity. He expended as much effort on a song of secondary or tertiary importance as upon one being groomed as a hit. When he completed a song that satisfied him no practical considerations tempted him into changing what he had written. He would be furious at arrangers who altered his own concepts of tempo, harmony, or rhythm. "Perhaps," explains Paul Weston, the conductor, "this is because Kern always 'composed' the melody—instead of setting some lyrics to music—and once he composed it, he found it very difficult to change an eighth note, even when he could greatly assist his lyricist in doing so."

During a rehearsal of a stage musical, early in his career, he suddenly rose from his seat, walked over to the musicians, and quietly collected the parts of one of his songs because it was being tampered with in performance. Later on in his career he became even more intransigent. When motion picture producers wanted certain structural changes in songs he wrote for them—which was not infrequent by any means—he always preferred to work out new numbers rather than revising the old ones. Once, when asked to adapt the range of a song to the gifts of a movie star, he replied sharply that it was much easier to change the star. Whenever alterations were suggested in his songs he would look icily at the Hollywood producer or director and ask in a steel-like voice: "Why?" As he once explained to the then still young inexperienced Paul Weston: "Young man, if you want to accomplish anything in this business you must remember that it is extremely important that you meet every suggestion with the word 'why?', and say it loudly and in an annoying manner. That way, you're a little ahead to start with, and in the end you'll get your way." And Kern always got his way.

Many have tried to imitate a Kern song but none have succeeded, because with Kern certain repetitious stylistic idiosyncrasies or individual technical methods cannot be copied. Only Kern himself had the gift to endow a simple diatonic or chromatic scale, within an elementary song form, with such enchanting moods and amazing inventiveness.

Perhaps the true secret of Kern's magic lies in the fact that the man and his song were one, the song being a mirror to the varied facets of his personality. If his songs provide such wonderful entertainment, perhaps it is because one of Kern's surpassing talents as a human being was his ability to entertain his friends continually with wonderful talk, wit, and culture. If those songs are seductive in their loveliness, perhaps it is because they have in them so much of Kern's own surpassing charm. In his songs we can find much of the joy of life, grace, worldly sophistication, and youthful enthusiasm that made Kern the kind of man he was.

Who, then, is this Jerome Kern?

2

A Man of Many Faces

He was something of a paradox.

He was a serious student of the theater, a musician of extraordinary gifts and achievement, a sophisticate, a man of the world who was extremely well-informed and well-read, a bon vivant with exquisite taste. He was the gracious host who always remembered and enjoyed catering even to the slightest interests of his guests. He was the charming companion whose conversation was usually scintillating; who could spend hours into the night (he always hated going to bed) in penetrating discussions of varied subjects, impressing his friends continually with a seemingly inexhaustible fund of information on many varied and sometimes even esoteric subjects. This was the Kern whom friends liked to describe as a college professor: a man of propriety, a man well-poised, sedate, and dignified. This was the Kern who dressed in conservative, well-tailored, and tastefully assembled clothes; who spoke in cultured accents, his sentences neatly rounded and his phrases well-turned. His head cocked to one side (a familiar pose), his usually puckish eyes behind owl-like spectacles would become soft and pensive. His lips, ordinarily touched with wit, would be pulled down at the corners; his jowls would sag to bring a sobriety of expression under the eyes. Over his mobile face, so often alight with roguish good humor, would pass varying subtle shades of reflection.

Then there was a second Kern in direct contradiction to the first. The other was the perpetual boy who refused to grow up. This Kern would abandon his more conservative clothes for flamboyant and outlandish costumes or special outfits. This, too, was the Kern with a lifelong passion for games of all sorts, puzzles, and schoolboy pranks.

The same intensity he brought to work, books, the stage, and cultural discussions, he could also carry to play: to such parlor games as Twenty Questions or Guggenheim, the latter a pencil and paper pastime sometimes known as Categories which he invented and which grew popular even out of his own circle; also to a quiz game, once again of his own concoction, in which pictures of famous people of history or current events, of art works, or of characters of plays and fiction had to be identified. He loved to gamble at poker, pinochle, bridge, roulette, and on the horses. Poker was a particular addiction. In the 1920's in New York he was a member of the famous Thanatopsis Literary and Inside Straight Club which included F.P.A., George S. Kaufman, Heywood Broun, Alexander Woollcott, and other literati of the Algonquin Hotel. A decade or so later he attended the Saturday evening poker sessions in Beverly Hills, about which more will be said in a later chapter. He always came to these games equipped with his checkbook—quietly and stoically accepting his inevitable losses. There were times when Kern's losses were such a foregone conclusion that the members of the Thanatopsis Club made a pool, its winner being the one best able to guess the amount Kern would lose that night. Nor was he any luckier in other games of chance. "It's a poor wheel," he once remarked about roulette, "that won't work both ways. And it must be the poor wheels that I keep playing."

His one-time appetite for baseball was schoolboyish in its insatiability. He rarely allowed a Saturday or Sunday to pass without being at the Polo Grounds, rooting for his beloved Giants. A boner by a member of that team reacted on him as a personal affront, and he would grow so grumpy and bitter that only numerous redeeming plays at bat and in the field could finally placate him. These visits to the Polo Grounds had become such a weekly ritual that when one Saturday he found both his cars in use and was unable to find a taxi he went to a local dealer and bought himself a new Essex in order not to miss the game.

Another interest, though by no means so passionate, was golf. He first took up golf seriously in the late 1910's when he was invited to play at a fashionable English course. He bought a special outfit for the occasion, memorized a book on golf techniques, and at his first effort made a perfect swing. Somewhat later he even managed to get a hole in one. Then he seemed to lose all interest in formal golf on traditional courses, and in Beverly Hills preferred to spend his golfing time putting about on a pitch and putt course.

But he never lost interest in doing the spontaneous and the unexpected. "Pixieish" or "puckish" are adjectives used most often by his friends to describe his quixotic bent to indulge impulsively in acts to startle or amuse them. But he liked even more to indulge in practical jokes and pranks. At a moment's whim he would deliver a pompous Temperance speech in a crowded subway or trolley car, even at the Polo Grounds. Late one night in Beverly Hills, spurred on by several of his guests (including George Gershwin, Harold Arlen, and Johnny Green), he stepped to the balcony of his eighth-floor suite at the Beverly-Wilshire Hotel and delivered his Temperance speech to a startled group emerging from the Brown Derby across the street.

On one occasion he was strolling in London with his wife and a few friends. Coming upon a group of workers busily engaged in building a foundation for a pavilion he told them with all the authority he could muster: "My good men, we've decided not to erect this building after all, so you can all go home." Which they did—to Kern's immense delight!

When *The Cat and the Fiddle* tried out in Philadelphia, Kern wrote a lewd sketch and conspired with several members of the cast to slip it deftly within the context of the play for a single rehearsal. His purpose was merely to startle the producer, Max Gordon, notorious for his aversion to stage obscenity. Gordon, indeed, was startled into a tantrum —much to Kern's joy, who finally confessed it had all been just a practical joke. When such tricks and pranks worked, Kern would chortle with delight or roar with laughter until the tears rolled down his cheeks, as he indulged in a favorite gesture expressing pleasure, that of rubbing his hands in his hair. He gave every appearance of having just pulled off a major coup.

There was also something essentially boyish in the way he used to collect things, though once launched on a collecting spree his approach became highly mature and professional. He would learn everything he could about the subject until he became both a connoisseur and an authority. Then he would spend a fortune on his hobby with seeming recklessness. Actually his purchases proved so shrewd that each of his collections, when disposed of, brought a huge profit over the original investment.

There was a time in the 1920's when he became an avid hunter of rare books, manuscripts, presentation copies, and so forth. The dealers early came to regard him as a "sucker," and as soon as he manifested an interest in some precious item the price was immediately raised by several thousand dollars. In time, his collection became a fabulous repository of first editions by Shelley, Coleridge, and Keats, among many others; the 1663 and 1664 issues of Shakespeare; original manuscripts by Tennyson, Swinburne, Samuel Johnson (the only existing page in manuscript from his *Dictionary*), and Oliver Goldsmith (the longest existing manuscript in handwriting); presentation or dedication copies of works by Burns, Robert Louis Stevenson, Coleridge, Kipling, Meredith, and Thackeray. When the possession of these treasures had become too much of a responsibility for him and he decided to dispose of them at a three-day public sale at the Anderson Galleries in January, 1929, his collection brought about two million dollars or approximately three times the amount he had originally expended. The very booksellers who once thought they had put over a sharp deal now scrambled over one another in their haste to buy back some of their own items at from two to ten times the original sales price. The Robert Burns presentation copy, for example, which had been marked up for Kern to $6,500 was sold for $23,000. (It was characteristic of Kern that a few minutes after the complete sale of his books had been consummated, he walked over to his favorite book dealer near the Anderson Galleries and purchased a few items for a new collection.)

At different times in his life Kern also collected stamps,

coins, and old silver. In the last category he amassed a precious collection of goblets and other drinking vessels, some still decorating the North Doheny Drive home of his daughter, Betty, in Beverly Hills. In order to get a better choice of imported silver pieces Kern set up a young friend in a shop at Rockefeller Center, financing the project without expecting or receiving any return on his investment.

One day, while strolling along Madison Avenue in New York, Kern saw a rare silver creamer of the Queen Anne period in the window of an antique shop. He paid an exorbitant price for it, but on bringing it to his young friend in Rockefeller Center he discovered it was a fraud. Kern demanded and received his money back. But a few weeks later he again saw the same piece in the window of the antique shop on Madison Avenue, still identified as a Queen Anne creamer. He grew so furious that he rushed over to the Antique Society to lodge a complaint; then he returned to the shop with a file to scratch away the false hallmark. Undoubtedly he would have proceeded from here to prosecute the shopkeeper and have his license revoked if in the next few weeks the dealer had not gone out of business.

This man, who could be a worldly sophisticate at one time and a boyish prankster at another, boasted still another glaring contradiction in his personality. He could be excessively considerate, affectionate, and generous; and he could also be cold and hard and calculating. He could be sensitive to the feelings of other people; but he could also be candid to a fault, speaking out with an almost brutal directness and often coating his remarks with stinging acid. Close friends would sometimes complain to him that he bullied them mercilessly and victimized them with his domineering ways. He would then grow contrite and quietly explain that, after all, he was considerate and affable only to those in whom he had no interest. He could love without reservation, but when he hated, he hated lustily. His anger, while short-lived, could be tempestuous. Exceptionally proud and sensitive, he often permitted small incidents to affect him out of all proportion to their importance.

He was a man of positive opinions, a man who did not like admitting he had made a mistake, a man who became inflexible once he had come to a decision. He had to be master of every situation. In any deal in which he was involved he had to feel he held the reins. People never directly told him what they wanted him to do, even for his own good, since his instinctive reaction would have been to balk at their suggestions. Instead they used strategy and guile to bring him around to their way of thinking. Even his business affairs were sometimes conducted in such a devious manner. If his attorney, Howard Reinheimer, had an offer from M-G-M for $100,000 for a Kern musical Reinheimer would not come right out and relay this offer to Kern, for he knew that Kern's first impulse would be to say the price was not right and he was not interested. Reinheimer's strategy would be to come to Kern and inquire coyly if it might not be a wise idea to sell this musical to M-G-M. Kern would probably agree, providing M-G-M stood ready to pay a reasonable price, say $75,000 or $100,000. Reinheimer would then suggest trying to make such a deal. A week later he would inform Kern that the deal had been made—always leaving with Kern the impression that the project and the price had originated with him.

Kern considered himself quite a businessman. This was probably the reason why he always strained to make a shrewd deal, even when small sums were involved. Nobody could accuse him of being parsimonious, since he spent his money lavishly on his way of life and was most extravagant with expensive gifts. As a matter of fact, he was unusually careless about money, never knew how much he had with him at any given time, and never argued over the price of anything he wanted to buy. But in any kind of business deal he could be as argumentative as a fishwife. An accountant—recommended to him for the examination of ledgers of a motion picture for which Kern was entitled to a percentage of the profits—insisted on a salary of $750 a week for services which would result for Kern in hundreds of thousands of dollars. But all Kern would pay him was $700. While working with Guy Bolton on an unproduced patriotic musical, *The Little Thing*, Bolton suggested to Kern that after all their years of collaboration he was finally entitled to an equal share of royalties. The difference to Kern in actual income would have been picayune; but in his own peculiar way Kern interpreted Bolton's request as an attack on his generosity, on his spirit of fair play, and on his friendship for Bolton. He curtly turned down this request, not only refusing to discuss this matter further, but even going so far as to refuse to work again with Bolton. When Ira Gershwin became his lyricist and also suggested a fifty-fifty split in song royalties, Kern would consider only a division of fifty-five per cent to himself and forty-five to Gershwin. Haggling of this kind, in which he was continually involved, seemed to be just one more game with him.

Kern placed a high value not only on his business acumen but also (and with complete justification) on his knowledge of real estate, architecture, and home decoration. Whenever one of his friends was engaged in any kind of construction or renovation or in the purchase of property, Kern would be put out if he were not consulted. To one such friend he once wrote with an equal blend of wit and peevishness:

Well, people will do these foolish things. I cannot understand it. Here am I, untrammeled by any studio commitments, doing nothing except pitching and putting, quite eager and willing to contribute my expert services; and yet, in spite of it all, Eddie Chodorov buys himself a house, Eddie Knopf rebuilds himself a house, Frank Mandel buys himself a house, and now you, all without so much as a smidge of consultation with the master. This short-sightedness just forces me to confine my talents to the oil business.

Beyond habits, interests, diversions, and idiosyncrasies already commented upon, Kern was extremely partial to old friends (to whom he remained attached until the end of his life), old hats, and to the use of a telephone. He was, of course, a habitual theatergoer. In the 1910's he also used to go to concerts, acquiring free tickets by writing unsigned reviews for the *Musical Courier;* but later on he preferred hearing good music on records or over the radio. He was fond of animals, particularly of his daughter's boxer, Sieglinde von Hirshfeld, who had won several ribbons and cups and to whom he would write letters when he was away from home. And he was always a devoted and dedicated husband to Eva, father to Betty, and grandfather to Steve.

His aversions included grand opera, night clubs, shams of any kind whether in commodities or in people, the word "cupid" in a song, and nail biters. He once promised motion picture producer Sam Marx, one of his song manuscripts if, in turn, Marx gave up the habit of biting his nails. Marx promised he would, becoming one of a mere handful of friends to own a Kern manuscript. (But Kern was exasperated to find Marx soon helplessly reverting to his old nail-biting habit!)

He loved to laugh. But even more than that he loved making those around him laugh, and for this he had a natural talent. He was a wonderful raconteur, a skillful teller of funny stories; he was deft at producing an unexpected answer to a simple question; he was quick with a pun or an amusing observation. When an Indian in Florida informed him she was one of the last Crees to be found there he remarked: "To be sure, *la derniére Cree.*" Oscar Hammerstein II once discussed with him the making of a musical comedy out of Donn Byrne's *Messer Marco Polo,* and inquired what kind of music Kern could write for a story laid in China about an Italian and written by an Irishman. Kern's answer was prompt: "Why, Jewish music, of course." One day, while standing at a curb outside a theater he noticed a glamorous show girl stepping from a handsome car. When he made some passing remark to her about her sudden affluence, she said: "Just for that, Jerry, next time I'll come in a Rolls Royce." "Oh, no!" Kern answered, "you won't get a Rolls Royce *just for that.*" And to an actress who liked emphasizing the "r's" in her speech, and who asked him how to cross a stage filled with props, he advised: "Just roll on your 'r's,' dearie."

For a man who was rigid in so many things and who had to produce so much work under a continual pressure of deadlines, Kern was unusually averse to routine and discipline of any kind. He never rose or went to bed at a set time and was inconsistent in his eating habits. He even refused to work when he did not feel like it. As Hammerstein recalls: "You might visit him on a certain afternoon all ready to pitch into work and find that he was in a mood to dawdle. He might have a new puzzle to work out, or he might feel like calling up a bookmaker and make bets on the races that day." When he did finally get down to the business of work he often made a game out of it. "We would act out our scenes and sing songs with great fervor, or humor, or whatever interpretation the material seemed to warrant," continued Hammerstein. "At one time we decided the best way to spend our lives would be to write plays that were never produced. We would never then entrust them to mere actors and singers whose portrayals couldn't possibly match our own—certainly not while we were in our own audience."

But though he might work sometimes in the morning or at other times in the afternoon and on still other occasions late at night (or many days not at all), he never failed to complete an assignment on time or have it measure up to his own strict standards. In fact, he usually completed more songs than were required or expected, since he liked to write alternate numbers for a single place in a play or picture. "Composing," he once said, "is like fishing. You get a nibble, but you don't know whether it's a minnow or a marlin until you reel it in. You write twenty tunes to get two good ones, and the wastebasket yearns for the music." Those that were not used but were too good for discard were put into a well-stocked file or notebook for later use.

Most of Kern's work was done at the piano, which was equipped with a working desk attached to the keyboard to facilitate writing. He often scribbled his melodies with pen and ink on the reverse side of used manuscripts that happened to be at hand. He would then try out the melodies at the keyboard. When he did not like what he had created, he would slam the palms of his hands on the keys and mutter violent oaths. Then he would start all over again. But when he produced something he liked he would rub his hair with excitement; or, after playing the song, would complete it with a resounding discord. Impatient to have his lyricist hear what he had done, when he was proud of the result, he would telephone him immediately (even across the country) and play the melody for him. Usually, however, the lyricist would receive the finished melody by recordings made in Kern's studio. Since Kern was in awe and afraid of complicated machinery, his daughter used to operate the recording devise for him. "Even a simple tool like a screwdriver gives me the chills," he confessed.

3

"Romie"

The first book Jerome Kern read was Mark Twain's *Adventures of Huckleberry Finn* (published in the year of Kern's birth). Mark Twain remained one of Kern's favorite writers, and was the inspiration for and the source of one of his two works for symphony orchestra.

It is possible that at least one reason for Kern's devotion to Mark Twain was the fact that his own father bore a physical resemblance to the writer. Kern brought to his parents, when they were alive—and to their memory afterward—a touching tenderness and depth of feeling. It is likely that at least subconsciously he always identified Mark Twain with his own father.

His father, Henry, was a short, lithe, energetic little man who earned a comfortable living as president of a firm which had the concession to sprinkle water on the city streets. That income was further supplemented by profits from periodic, successful operations in real estate. Jerome Kern, consequently, was born to and raised in an upper-middle-class home.

Henry Kern had been born in Baden-Baden, Germany, but raised in New York, where he met Fanny Kakeles, an American of Bohemian ancestry whose family had included several members of nobility. Fanny's father was a beadle at Temple Emanu-El, New York—a man of dignified bearing, with fine features, commanding nose and eyes, and an impressive Vandyke beard. The esteem with which Jerome Kern regarded him may be gathered from the fact that to this day the old man's stern features look down from a painting on the dining-room wall of the Jerome Kern house in Beverly Hills. Such high esteem notwithstanding, the grandfather's strong religious convictions could not percolate down to his son-in-law, Henry, let alone to his grandson, Jerome. There was little consciousness of formal religion within the Henry Kern household. As for Jerome, though he always acknowledged his Jewish birth, he was all his life completely divorced from the Hebrew ritual.

Jerome's mother, Fanny, was a small, slim woman with sensitive features, and extraordinarily attractive physically. She was a highly social and gregarious woman who loved giving regal parties and dinners. She was also a woman of culture, and an excellent amateur pianist, who contributed to the Kern home both intellectual grace and refinement, just as her husband provided the physical comforts. In the Kern ménage there was always music, talk of the theater and of books, a profound respect for education—and elegant dinners.

Henry and Fanny Kern had nine children, all boys. Only three survived. Joseph, the oldest of the three, became a builder, and like his father dabbled in real estate. Edwin, who came next, at one time owned a record and sheet music shop. When Jerome, the last of the nine males, was born, Fanny had prayed desperately for a girl. In his early years she dressed him in Little Lord Fauntleroy suits and lace collars, and trained his hair to dangle in rows of curls, as is revealed by a daguerreotype taken when Jerome was about three.

Jerome David Kern (he clung to the middle name until the middle 1900's, then discarded it for good) was born at 411 East 56th Street, New York, where the Kerns resided at the time, on January 27, 1885. The day he was born, his mother and father had spent the afternoon at the races. They were motoring home from the upper Bronx when, passing Jerome Avenue, the mother was seized with her first labor pains. It is for this reason she decided to call her son Jerome.

Jerome Kern's boyhood was spent not on East 56th Street, but a little further uptown: on East 74th Street, between Park and Lexington Avenues, where Henry Kern purchased a commodious three-floor graystone house. It was there that his mother introduced him to the piano, when he was only five. Something of a frustrated musician herself, she was determined to make him a prodigy. When placed in front of a piano this kind and gentle soul acquired the hard crust of a martinet who would continually strike the boy's knuckles with a ruler when his fingers were not in proper position or when they slipped to a wrong note. So often was the child smitten that the keyboard became scarred and the ivory on the keys cracked. But apparently this rigid regimen did not dampen the boy's enthusiasm for the piano. He was continually improvising, continually making up little tunes to his own simple tonic-dominant accompaniments. He even enjoyed dull and routine exercises.

The mother's severity with his music lessons was fortunately generously tempered with the overwhelming love and solicitude with which she surrounded him at all other times. She had good reason to be particularly devoted to him. In 1884, a year before Jerry was born, she lost two of her sons; and a third died in 1889 when Jerry was only four. Her youngest, then, would have occupied a special niche in her heart—even if he did not possess a lovable nature which continually won the affection of all with whom he came into contact. His soft and sensitive personality—to which malice of any kind seemed alien—made him more considerate of the feelings of others than children usually are. And he continually betrayed an endearing sense of fun and was a perpetual geyser of enthusiasms. He consequently became the favorite of the family, on whom the Kern parents showered their favors. He always had plenty of spending money in his pockets. He was allowed a freedom of activity, movement, and decision few of his friends enjoyed. Such freedom proved significant in his development as a musician: his parents, who never had the heart to deny him anything, could not even make token objection when, after he had completed high school, he preferred to abandon formal academic schooling and to avoid the business world for the sake of music.

Kern's greatest single life disappointment was the fact that neither of his parents lived to see him achieve a commanding place in music (though they did live long enough to see him attain some measure of financial security from music). Fanny Kern died of cancer on December 31, 1907. This is the reason why, as long as he lived, Jerome Kern never celebrated New Year's Eve. On August 31, 1908, less than a year after Fanny's death, Henry Kern was a victim of pernicious anemia. Both were buried in Salem Fields Cemetery in Jamaica, New York. Kern paid regular visits to their graves; such a visit took place only one day before his own sudden and fatal cerebral attack.

When Jerry attended a private kindergarten and the local public schools he outgrew his curls, lace collars, and Little Lord Fauntleroy suits. But throughout his boyhood there was something pleasantly effeminate about him: in the delicate features of his face, and particularly of the lips; in the gentleness of his eyes; in the softness of his personality; and in the remarkable clarity of his skin, which for the most part remained free from such boyhood blemishes as pimples, blackheads, or acne. But the neighborhood boys, to whom he was always known as "Romie," never seemed to resent or abuse him for his feminine looks and ways. Boys such as Willie Kahn, David Friend, and Maurice Wolff welcomed him to their street games: nine o' cat, duck on the rock, roller skating, playing with pinwheels which they themselves fabricated from varnished colored paper. He frequently joined them at Rappaport's toy store on 79th Street where they liked to loiter and to which they consigned so much of their spending money.

Yet he was different from his friends in several ways. He was extremely imaginative, given to spinning fanciful tales which he presented as the truth—much to the exasperation of the maid in the Kern household who one day threatened to quit if the boy did not desist from continually fooling her with his tall stories. He liked to wander off to the Episcopal church a mile uptown to listen to choir practice. And he found the piano not only an inexhaustible source of pleasure but even the medium for perpetrating little pranks and tricks, a weakness to which he was already strongly addicted. One of the ways he entertained his friends was by playing the piano with back turned to the keyboard, his hands pursuing a sprightly tune behind his back. Or he would lie down on the floor in front of the piano, play the keys with upstretched hands, and use his shoulders to manipulate the pedals.

By the time he was ten he started going to the Broadway theater. The musical stage instantly proved a heady experience. Maurice Wolff recalls late one afternoon in 1895, when playing outside his house he saw Jerry Kern pass him by in a state of unusual agitation. When he asked Kern what had happened, the boy urged Wolff to come home with him. There Kern confided he had just been to a matinee performance of Victor Herbert's *The Wizard of the Nile*, and proceeded to describe for Wolff some of the amusing shenanigans of Frank Daniels as Kibosh, the magician of ancient Egypt. Then Kern went over to the piano and played by ear some of the Herbert tunes he had just heard, especially the lilting waltz, "Starlight, Star Bright." "I was on pins and needles as 'Romie' talked and played, because I was afraid I'd get home late for dinner," Wolff recalls. "But I couldn't help being fascinated by his exciting enthusiasm and by the way he played the piano."

In that same year of 1895 the Kerns moved to Newark, New Jersey, where the father acquired control of the merchandizing house of D. Wolf & Co. In Newark, Kern completed his elementary schooling, then went on to the Barringer High School. There his musical gifts were noticed and first given recognition. He was asked to play the piano or organ at the school assemblies. He wrote music for school productions; some of these tunes later being adapted to new lyrics for his first Broadway musicals. His teachers used to refer to him as "the little genius," and were tolerant of his less distinguished scholastic accomplishments. "As a matter of fact," Kern confided many years later, "they let me get away with murder."

In June 1902, Kern was graduated from high school, and that summer he worked for his father. One of the deals in which he became involved almost spelled financial disaster for the merchandizing house. Sent to New York to purchase two pianos Kern visited a piano factory on 138th Street owned by an Italian. The Italian took him to his home and with typical Latin expansiveness forced on Kern an ample Italian dinner and several glasses of Chianti. Flattered by this attention, charmed by his host's graciousness, and a bit heady with wine, Kern inquired from the Italian how many pianos he had in his warehouse. When informed there were two hundred Kern proceeded to buy the whole lot. Fortunately, Kern's father was ultimately able to devise a shrewd installment plan whereby the pianos could be disposed of and even yield a handsome profit for the firm. (This episode surely must have reminded Father Kern of an incident in which he himself had been involved many years earlier. A devotee of auctions, Henry Kern once fell asleep at one, and while asleep, nodded his head vigorously. Upon awakening he discovered he had purchased a carload of prunes.)

If Henry Kern had any further doubts on the subject, they were permanently dispelled by Jerry's piano deal. Jerry was no business tycoon. That fall, Jerry enrolled in Normal College in New York (later Hunter College Training School), and at the same time he entered the New York College of Music for further study. At the latter place, he studied piano with Alexander Lambert, Albert von Doenhoff, and Paolo Gallico, and harmony with Austen Pearce. Years after Kern had become famous Gallico used to recall at The Bohemians club his experiences teaching Kern piano; Gallico insisted that if Kern had been so disposed and had prepared himself properly he would have distinguished himself in serious music. But the concert world had little appeal to young Kern. Already he was busy scribbling popular tunes which he started circulating in Tin Pan Alley. One of these actually managed to find a publisher: a slight piano piece in 6/8 moderato time called "At the Casino," with a rippling melody in triplets in a humdrum rhythm and formal harmonies. Lyceum Publishing Company published it on September 5, 1902, in a flashy bright red, gray, and white cover depicting a casino.

Kern continued his music study for a year. Then, in the fall of 1903, he persuaded his father to finance a trip to Europe.

4

From Tin Pan Alley to Shubert Alley

Kern stayed in Europe about a year. Part of the time was spent in Germany, gathering musical impressions and experiences and taking lessons in theory and composition from private teachers in Heidelberg. He was strongly impressed by the city of Heidelberg, became fond of Bavaria, and disliked Berlin. During most of his European visit, however, Kern lived in London where he soon found a song writing assignment in the office of Charles Frohman, the American producer, then equally active on both the Broadway and London stages. Kern's duties were as humble as his less than two-pounds-a-week salary. At that time London musicals habitually presented their least important songs (generally the work of hacks) at the start of each performance. The reason for this was that London audiences generally came late, and these numbers merely served the utilitarian purpose of providing fill-in material until the audience arrived and the main performers could be presented. It was these numbers that Kern was hired to write. The first was "My Little Canoe," which Billie Burke (then only seventeen, making her first public appearance as a singer) presented in *The School Girl* at the Pavilion Music Hall in the winter of 1903. Here, as in many other songs by Kern written at this time, he imitated the easy, graceful, light Continental style of London's popular operetta composer, Leslie Stuart, famous for *Florodora* and *The Silver Slipper.*

Some of Kern's songs were also used in several Frohman musicals featuring Seymour Hicks at the Aldwych theater. Hicks liked Kern's melodies and was responsible for bringing the young composer to the attention of a brilliant young columnist of the *Globe*, Pelham Grenville Wodehouse. Wodehouse was twenty-four, a graduate of Dulwich College where he had attracted considerable attention and inspired mirth by writing satires on his fellow students in Greek verse. Wodehouse's relatives convinced him to consider a career in banking. For a while Wodehouse worked as a clerk in several London banking houses. But all the while he was scribbling amusing verses and stories; some sold to small journals and newspapers. After two years of banking Wodehouse decided to try to make his way as a writer. Almost immediately he became popular in London for his amusing pieces, especially those appearing in his regular column in the *Globe*, "By the Way," which he started in 1903.

Seymour Hicks, needing a topical song with several encore verses, offered Wodehouse three pounds to write one. Hicks also suggested young Kern from the Frohman office as a likely candidate for the music. Wodehouse's first meeting with Kern took place at the Aldwych theater to which

Wodehouse had come during rehearsal to discuss his lyric with Kern. Kern was in shirt-sleeves, playing poker with several actors. "When I finally managed to free him from the card table and was able to talk with him," Wodehouse recalls, "I became impressed. Here, I thought, was a young man supremely confident of himself, the kind of person who inspires people to seek him out when a job must be done."

The song Wodehouse and Kern wrote was "Mr. Chamberlain," a timely political piece—Chamberlain being none other than the distinguished English statesman, Joseph Chamberlain, leader of the Liberal Unionists and father of Neville who became England's prime minister just before World War II. Seymour Hicks sang "Mr. Chamberlain" (together with two other Kern numbers) in *The Beauty of Bath,* and scored such a hit that for the next year "Mr. Chamberlain" was one of London's most popular tunes.

Hicks may have been indebted to Kern for a successful song, but he soon was unkindly disposed to Kern as a man. In one of his pretentious attitudes Hicks presented Kern with a handsome enlarged photograph of himself, appropriately inscribed. In his first visit to Kern Hicks discovered that Kern had hung the picture in his bathroom.

The English actor, George Grossmith (later a member of the circle of Kern's most intimate friends, a frequent, visitor to Kern's home both in London and New York), first met Kern during this period, though in his autobiography, *G.G.,* he erroneously places the date several years ahead.

> I knew him as Jerry Kern and liked him immensely. He often came to my house and played to us. He played divinely . . . with a tremendous gift of "tune." He was the only one I could detect in a barren field likely to fill the shoes of Lionel Monckton, Paul Rubens, and Leslie Stuart. In my dressing room at the Gaiety was a tiny yacht piano

on which Rubens had composed his first song. . . . "Give me a lyric," one night asked Jerry, "and let me try what I can do on the same instrument." Together we wrote and composed "Rosalie," which I sang in, I think, *The Spring Chicken*. . . . Kern wrote several things for George Edwardes (manager of the Gaiety) but had no outstanding success.

Back in New York in 1904, Kern sought to make his way into the Broadway theater by way of Tin Pan Alley. His first job was with the same organization which had published "At the Casino" three years earlier, the Lyceum Publishing Company, his salary, seven dollars a week. Since there was no place for him on the musical staff he was required to make out the bills and invoices. Kern did not remain there long, having found a nine dollar a week job, this time as a song plugger with Shapiro-Remick Company; he worked in five-and-ten cent stores in the city, and at times in Wanamaker's department store in Philadelphia, demonstrating songs published by his firm.

While plying the menial trade of song plugger Kern received his first opportunity to write music for the Broadway theater. The producer, Edward E. Rice, had imported from England *Mr. Wix of Wickham*, which he presented at the Bijou in New York on September 19, 1904, with a cast including Harry Corson Clarke and Thelma Fair. *Mr. Wix of Wickham* was a dish that had been reheated several times in England before being served to American audiences, and in the process it had lost much of its savor. "Surely," commented the New York *Dramatic Mirror*, "its last state is worse than the first." The play was an innocuous, meandering comedy set in Australia, where Mr. Wix of Wickham, England, ran a shop and was duped by practical jokers into believing he is the missing heir to a fortune; the real heir proves to be a young man who had fallen in love with a girl working in the Wix establishment.

Kern's job was to adapt the original English score by Herbert Darnley and George Everard. And Kern's contribution was one of the few redeeming features of a sorry production —bringing such fresh harmonization and instrumentation to the English score that Alan Dale had to sit up and take notice. Kern also placed four of his own songs into the play, one being particularly intriguing for its bounce and buoyancy, "Waiting for You," introduced by Harry Corson Clarke.

While working for Shapiro-Remick, Kern became a friend of Ernest R. Ball. In the next few years Ball would become one of America's most famous creators of ballads. In 1905 he was still a staff pianist for the house of Witmark which had just published his first song hit to Walker's lyrics, "Will You Love Me in December as You Do in May?". Ball sold Kern on the idea of trying to get a job with Harms, one of the more dynamic and progressive young publishing houses in Tin Pan Alley, due to the perspicacity of its acting head, Max Dreyfus. Kern made his way to 44th Street, where Harms then occupied a high-stoop brownstone house, and was ushered into Dreyfus' office. Kern noticed immediately (and was duly impressed) that Dreyfus was wearing a Prince Albert coat and striped trousers, while near him on the table reposed a high silk hat. This elegant attire convinced Kern that the house of Harms had genuine "class," and that a man who wore such dress to work was the kind of person he wanted to be associated with. What Kern did not know, but learned much later, was that Dreyfus was dressed that way that day because he was about to attend a funeral.

Dreyfus remembers that first interview with Kern. He

saw before him a slight, dark-haired, blue-eyed, eager young man with winning self assurance. "He said he wanted to imbibe the atmosphere of music," remembers Dreyfus. "I decided to take him on, and to start him off by giving him the toughest job I know, selling music." Kern was offered twelve dollars a week. Besides selling sheet music up Hudson Valley, Kern had to play Harms' songs in various stores, including Macy's, and do some of the house arrangements. "He was good," continues Dreyfus. "He was full of youthful spirit, and with it a certain charm. He sold music."

Kern was able to supplement his income by working as Marie Dressler's accompanist on the vaudeville stage, and occasionally by acting as rehearsal pianist for Broadway musicals. He was also drawing some royalties from songs which Dreyfus was already publishing. One of the first of these was also Kern's first American hit, "How'd You Like to Spoon With Me?". From then on, and until his death, Kern had his songs published by Harms. He not only soon became one of its star composers but in time also one of its top executives.

As the first American song hit of one of our foremost song writers, "How'd You Like to Spoon With Me?" deserves special attention. Edward Laska, a successful composer and lyricist in the early 1900's, had been commissioned to write a song for two overweight performers. He conceived the amusing idea of writing a lyric for two fat people which would burlesque the traditional love duet and be built around the word "spoon." Having met Kern several times at Harms, and having become aware of his talent, Laska asked him to write the music. Laska found him at Harms "with a straw hat on, of which the top was knocked off, and a long black cigar in his mouth being 'cold-smoked.'" Laska goes on to explain: "I don't think I ever really saw him smoke one, but it seemed to inspire him as he ground out melody after melody without bothering to jot them down." Laska told Kern the title of his projected lyric, outlined the main idea, and suggested its basic rhythm. "At once, as though it were a song he had known all his life, he improvised a tune that fit exactly."

There is good reason to doubt that Kern improvised the melody quite as spontaneously as Laska thought. Kern's cousin, Walter Pollak—who had been intimate with Kern from boyhood on—insists that the melody of "How'd You Like to Spoon With Me?" was one Kern had written for a high school production in Newark. Pollak had seen that school play and clearly remembers hearing the tune there.

When Kern and Laska presented their song to the producer who had commissioned it, the latter suggested changing the word "spoon," since he wanted to use the song in England for Edna May and in England the word "spoon" was virtually unknown. This idea appealed neither to Kern nor to Laska. They made a discreet exit and went over to the offices of the Shuberts atop the Lyric theater. By creating a fiction that he had been sent by Reginald De Koven—the successful and wealthy composer of *Robin Hood* and numerous other operettas—Kern managed to gain direct access to the Shubert brothers. They liked the song and decided to place it in their next production: Ivan Caryll's *The Earl and the Girl*, in which Eddie Foy was starred as a dog trainer hired to impersonate an earl. "Out on the street," Laska recalls, "we kids slapped one another over the back and I think we gleefully went into an apothecary's to have a couple of ice cream sodas. We hardly could realize that we were to have a featured song in a forthcoming Casino theater production."

The show tried out in Chicago. Kern, who was present,

wrote back excitedly to Laska that their song (given a serious rather than burlesque treatment) was a hit. After *The Earl and the Girl* opened in New York in the then recently remodeled and reopened Casino theater on November 4, 1905, "How'd You Like to Spoon With Me?" became the play's "swinging sensation," as an advertisement of the time referred to it. The New York *Dramatic Mirror* described it as "the most successful number ever introduced here; it was demanded again and again." In melodic content and structure this song was not much different—nor, for that matter, much better—than the kind of love duets frequently presented in New York. But it profited from an infectious presentation by Georgia Caine and Victor Morley, who were followed by six girls singing on flower-decorated swings as they floated from the stage into the audience. The song also became exceedingly popular in England where it was introduced in the *London Gaieties;* from then on the word "spoon" entered into the argot of the average Englishman.

With "How'd You Like to Spoon With Me?" Kern established significant contact with the Shuberts. During the next dozen years Kern placed many songs in Shubert productions. But at the same time he did not hesitate to re-establish his relations with his one-time London employer, Charles Frohman. Since Frohman was one of Broadway's most active producers and since he had always been kindly disposed to the young composer, Kern found many opportunities both to work as a rehearsal pianist for Frohman musicals and occasionally to interpolate his songs in them. The first Frohman production in which Kern songs appeared (three) was *Catch of the Season,* with Edna May starring at Daly's theater on August 28, 1905. From then on at least one of Kern's songs, and usually several, sprouted in virtually each of Frohman's musicals. Nor was Kern at all reticent in using his job as rehearsal pianist as a convenient means of getting his songs used. Before a rehearsal would begin, Kern would start playing one of his numbers, aimlessly and with seeming spontaneity. His hope was that it would catch the ear and possibly the fancy of either Frohman or one of the stars who might then insist that it be introduced into the show.

The interpolation of songs into musical productions was a widely prevalent practice in the American theater in the early part of the twentieth century. In the 1900's and 1910's this was particularly true of imported foreign operettas to which the American stage was then so strongly addicted. Such a practice was but part of the tradition of the times which dictated that the songs, dances, and humor need not be basic to the over-all text. A musical's function was to stimulate eye and ear, not the mind; and most musicals of the day were planned exclusively with concern for the effect performers, songs, dance routines, amusing episodes, lavish sets and costumes, and stunning stage effects had upon audiences. Plots, dramatic truth, characterizations, authentic atmosphere, credibility of action, integration of the various elements of good theater—all this was incidental. Thus if at any time before or during the run of a musical the producer came upon anything which might enhance the entertainment quotient of the play he did not hesitate to introduce it into the production at some convenient point, whether or not it had any relevance within the context.

In the early 1920's most important stage composers began introducing into their contracts a provision forbidding the use of interpolated musical material. But in the preceding two decades even famous composers like Victor Herbert and Sigmund Romberg were tolerant to this strange procedure, whereby the music of other men was grafted upon their own scores. This custom worked to the advantage of the unknown composer who found many opportunities to place songs either in musicals about to be produced or in those already running on Broadway. Many leading Broadway composers made their bow, and gained their experience, in this way, long before they had the opportunity to write stage scores of their own.

In the case of Kern it was eight years after *Mr. Wix of Wickham* before he received his first assignment to write a complete score of his own. But in all that time, Kern did not lack a showcase for his tunes. For many years the interpolation of his songs into productions by other composers gave him an intensive apprenticeship which proved all-important in his development as a composer for the stage. That apprenticeship provided him with a consummate knowledge of the stage—its demands, techniques, and practices—which would serve him well through the years. That knowledge taught him audience reaction, a lesson which made it possible for him to become as expert a showman as he was a technician in the writing of show tunes.

However, having songs interpolated into the musicals of other composers was not an unmixed blessing, as Kern soon discovered. Sometimes these songs were placed after the show had begun its run, thus failing to attract the attention of critics. Or, as happened on more than one occasion, a critic admiring a Kern song would frequently erroneously credit it to the composer of the basic score.

Between 1905 and 1912, Kern had almost a hundred songs interpolated in approximately thirty Broadway musicals. These plays included importations of foreign opperettas by Ivan Caryll and Lionel Monckton, Paul Rubens, Sidney Jones, Edmund Eysler, Leslie Stuart, Ludwig Englander, Oskar Straus, Leo Fall, and Emmerich Kálmán—

including the American premières of Straus' *A Waltz Dream* in 1908 and Leo Fall's *The Dollar Princess* in 1909, two classics of the European operetta theater.

These plays starred some of the leading performers of the American stage of that period: Julia Sanderson, Nora Bayes, Hattie Williams, Billie Burke, Edna May, Sam Bernard, Marie Doro, Eddie Foy, Trixie Friganza, Edna Wallace Hopper, John E. Hazzard, and Louise Dresser. Some of these musicals introduced to the American stage the famous female impersonator, Julian Eltinge, and the fabulous blackface minstrel, Al Jolson; they helped bring Violet Heming to New York, and Mae West to musical comedy.

From the mountain of songs produced by Kern for these varied productions only a few command interest. But these few already begin to suggest something of the cultured manner, the easy flow of melody, and the American idiomatic style of the mature Kern: "I'd Like to Meet Your Father" presented by Julia Sanderson in *The Dairy Maids;* the "Bagpipe Serenade," a delightful interlude by Georgia Caine and a group of girls dressed in kilts in *The Rich Mr. Hoggenheimer,* a production that also featured a winning song-and-dance routine by Flossie Hope and Carrie Bowman in "Poker Love"; and "Come On Over Here," a breezy trio from *The Woman Haters.*

5

Eva

By 1910 Jerome Kern had become the urbane young man whose life in the New York theater had brought him polish and sophistication, even as his occasional excursions to England to help produce songs for the London stage gave him some of the suave attitudes of a man of the world. From his music he was now receiving a yearly income in five figures, and was living accordingly. He occupied comfortable bachelor quarters at 107 West 68th Street, attended to by a faithful maid, Mary. He dressed in the latest fashion, but always with restraint and in the best taste. He entertained his New York and London friends in style, both at his apartment and in fashionable restaurants. He also passed lightly from one romance to another, generally with show girls; women always found him to be physically attractive as well as a charming and amusing companion. One love affair before his marriage involved him more deeply than all the others: in 1908, with Edith Kelly, a slight, vivacious, sexually provocative show girl. One reason given for his failure to marry was that he had once promised his parents never to marry a show girl, and Kern was not the man to take such a promise lightly. But it is possible that Edith, on the hunt for game richer than a song writer, rejected him. In 1909 she married tycoon Frank Jay Gould.

Numerous newspaper and magazine accounts have created a fiction about the way in which Kern first met his wife. Such a distortion of biographical truth would not even deserve passing comment here but for the fact that the fiction refuses to die. Guy Bolton (who should know better and probably does) repeated the legend in "Recollections of Jerome Kern," an article in the New York *Times*.

The story goes something like this. While in his hotel room in London Kern was haunted by a beautiful melody which he could not put down on paper since no piano was handy. When he heard the sound of piano playing in the adjoining room he knocked at the door to inquire if he might use the piano for a few minutes. He was met by a very young and attractive English girl with whom he immediately fell in love and whom he married soon afterward. A romantic episode, no doubt, but one that simply never took place. Let it be hoped that from this time on it will be consigned to permanent and well-deserved rest.

Actually the truth is both stranger and more fascinating than the fiction. While still reacting to the impact of his romance with Edith Kelly, Kern visited England in the summer of 1908 as a guest of Jimmy Blakely, an English actor who occupied a small bungalow near the Thames. One day Blakely took Kern to meet his friend, George Draper Leale, manager of the Swan hotel in Walton-on-Thames, thirty or so miles from London. En route to the hotel in their car Blakely waved to a girl passing by on a bicycle. "That's Eva,

George's seventeen-year-old daughter," Blakely told Kern. Later the same day Eva stepped into the Leale parlor to greet the visitors and be introduced to Kern. Then, with adolescent impetuousness and diffidence, she fled from the room. Kern had not failed to remark how appealing she was physically; fresh and radiant with youth. Nor had he failed to be impressed by the delicacy of her features which almost suggested the fragile, and her innocence of manner which touched the ingenuous.

Eva, oldest of the three Leale children, was born in London on June 17, 1891. Her father was a licensed victualer, who during her early childhood owned a London pub. (His second cousin, Dr. Charles Leale, had studied and practiced medicine in the United States and had attended Abraham Lincoln after the fatal shot at Ford's Theater. Dr. Leale's photograph appears in Stefan Lorant's *Lincoln: A Picture History of His Life.*) As a child, Eva (though Episcopalian) attended a Catholic kindergarten in London. After that she went to a grammar school in Lewisham where her father had acquired a pub, a venture in which he lost all his money when Eva was about fifteen. Having to take on a job he now became the manager of Swan hotel in Walton-on-Thames. Eva helped him by fixing grates, opening up the taproom, and waiting on the tables. Nevertheless, hers was such a completely sheltered life that even at seventeen she had never had a beau. Like a young Brünnhilde protected by a ring of flame, Eva was guarded by a strict father from the world outside his inn. Such overprotectiveness inevitably made of her a timid, self-conscious, and frightened little girl. At first sight Kern represented to her the personification of all her girlhood dreams. He was handsome, well-poised, cultured, witty, seemingly prosperous, and obviously gifted;

he was famous in London and New York. Eva fell in love at first sight.

That love affair was a page from a stuffy mid-Victorian novel. Kern often visited the Leales at Swan hotel, ostensibly to exchange tales and drink ale with George but actually to catch further glimpses of Eva. Sometimes he played the piano. "I had never heard such piano playing in my life," she says, "and as he played I would float off into another world." But Kern could find few opportunities to see her alone or to talk with her. She would flit in and out of the parlor with the elusiveness of a butterfly. She rarely said anything when she was in the room, keeping her head lowered, and only occasionally stealing a hasty glance at him. Their meetings under the most circumscribed circumstances usually lasted only a few minutes. That entire season Kern did not see her more than a dozen hours altogether. Yet he soon recognized that he was in love with her. During one of the rare occasions when he was alone with her he made a sudden gesture as if to take her in his arms and kiss her, but just as suddenly he changed his mind. "I sensed he wanted to kiss me, and I kept praying he would. When he didn't, I thought I would die of disappointment." Once, and only once, did he kiss her. This happened while she was reading the Sunday newspaper in the hotel garden. "He was," she confesses, "the first man who had ever kissed me, besides my relatives, and at the time I swore to myself he would be the last."

Another time when they were alone together she hummed "How'd You Like to Spoon With Me?". When Kern asked her the name of the tune she told him it was a song by some popular English composer. Kern finally revealed he was its composer, only to enrage her, since she felt he was trying to impress her by expropriating somebody else's song. When she became convinced that Kern had told her the truth he became in her eyes an even more glamorous and unattainble hero than he had heretofore been.

One day, in place of his now usual visit, Eva received from Kern a wire saying, "Leaving for New York tomorrow. Will see you next year. Love. Jerry." It was the first wire she had ever received and she treasured it, especially for the word "love" which she read and reread a dozen times. But her father grew furious that Kern had presumed to communicate directly with her without first asking permission. He insisted sternly that henceforth he must be shown any future correspondence between them. A few months later Kern sent Eva a long letter. Her father, once again aroused that Kern should dare write to Eva without first consulting him, finally and reluctantly gave her permission to reply but only if she showed him what she had written. This was the first time Eva perpetrated a deception on her father. After he had read her polite and discreet letter she slipped into the envelope a more intimate and endearing note. The exchange of letters continued for several months. Occasionally she succeeded in intercepting one of them before it reached her father, and sometimes she was able to make a secret response.

Then, one day in 1910, Kern wrote Eva's father asking permission to marry her. It took the father a month to answer affirmatively, upon which Kern wired Eva he was leaving immediately for England. He arrived at the Swan hotel long past midnight and was welcomed by Eva's father. Then Eva herself was permitted to come down from her room to greet her future husband. They did not rush into each other's arms. Instead, Kern asked her simply: "Are you ready to marry me?" She nodded quickly, unable to speak and petrified with fear that then and there, even at the zero hour, her father might raise some unreasonable objection.

After the calling of the banns, Jerome Kern married Eva Leale in a simple church ceremony in Walton on October 25, 1910. Their best man was Laurie de Freece, one of Kern's English actor friends; the maid of honor was another of Kern's London friends, Mabel Sealby. Then, after several weeks of honeymoon in London where they visited the White City Exhibition, the Kerns set sail for Eva's new homeland, the United States.

Even today Eva has little hesitancy in confessing that her marriage to Kern—wonderful though it was—had a shattering impact upon her from which she did not recover for many years. She felt completely inadequate for the *galant*, this worldlywise gentleman, this highly talented composer who had become her husband. She was in awe of him, and haunted perpetually by fears that some other woman, more sophisticated than she, might win him away from her. She was also in terror of the society into which she was so suddenly plunged. Being uprooted from a sheltered home in a small English town had given her a sense of insecurity which intensified her natural timidity to a point where she was hounded by fears she could not explain. She still remembers the terror that seized her when, upon first arriving in the United States, she waited for her husband in Max Dreyfus' office. Suddenly she felt she was in a strange, huge, alien world.

Her initial experiences in the new country did not contribute to her self-assurance. Her first shock was to discover that they did not even have a home to come to. The bachelor apartment on West 68th Street to which Kern brought her straight from the ship was occupied by three out-of-work actors to whom Kern had loaned the place during his absence, and who refused to get out because they had nowhere to go. The Kerns had to occupy a room in a nearby hotel for ten days until the actors could be prevailed upon to leave; and when they left, the apartment was a shambles. Somewhat later, after Eva had settled in the apartment and had created order out of chaos, she was consistently put out by the maid, Mary, first because Mary terrified her (Eva had never before seen a colored woman), and then because Mary had a sense of independence, pride, and a feeling of proprietary rights over Kern which no English domestic of Eva's experience would dare assume. One day, coming home from shopping, Eva was flabbergasted to find Mary in the living room playing the piano as if she were the mistress of the place; and she was further flustered to find her husband amused at her reaction and quietly tolerant of Mary's behavior. The fact that Mary herself was none too sympathetic to Eva did not help matters either; Mary had so long taken care of Kern when he had been a bachelor that she continually betrayed the fact she regarded Eva as an intruder.

At that, Eva herself could not overcome the uncomfortable feeling she was an intruder—an intruder in her home, in her husband's life, in America. There were all kinds of subtle and at times complex nuances of living in New York City with a successful composer which were completely alien to her and left her both disturbed and perplexed.

All her life Eva has remained a woman of exceptional reticence who has clung with desperate tenacity to the background of her husband's lustrous career. Except for Christmas, she rarely entertained in more than a perfunctory manner, and when she did entertain the experience always proved unnerving. During all the years she lived in or near

New York she never accompanied Kern to the out-of-town tryouts of his shows; she rarely associated with his colleagues of the theater; she knew almost nothing of his business affairs. She disliked going to parties and functions to which he was continually invited, so that Kern often went without her and people everywhere began accepting this as standard operating procedure with the Kerns. (When Kern's daughter, Betty, grew up he used to take her to these parties.)

Perhaps Eva was not completely to blame for this strange reserve and self-containment. The truth was that Kern wanted her to be that way. For all his worldliness there was something old-fashioned about the way Kern relegated her to the home, while keeping his own career and business affairs in a world apart.

During her first eighteen months in the United States Eva lived in Kern's bachelor apartment on West 68th Street. Then for another year and a half they set up a home of their own in more spacious quarters on West 70th Street between Broadway and West End Avenue. Eva did her own housework and made the frequently painful adjustments, not only to the American way of life but also to Kern's. She soon learned not to disturb him when he was at the piano working, nor to ply him with questions about his affairs. She respected his privacy in all such matters because she early came to realize that this was the way he wanted it—and in respecting his privacy scrupulously she receded more and more into a protective shell of her own.

6

Victor Herbert's Mantle

Kern was making broad forward strides within the Broadway theater. One of the musicals, in which he shared the score with Frank Tours by contributing seven numbers helped to open a new Taj Mahal of musical productions in New York: the Winter Garden, on March 20, 1911. This musical, *La Belle Paree*, was an extravaganza described on the program as a "Cook's tour through vaudeville with a Parisian landscape," and was part of a program that also included a Chinese-like opera. It was in *La Belle Paree*, and with several of Kern's songs, that Al Jolson made his stage debut—appropriately enough at the opening of a theater in which he would score his greatest personal triumphs.

A single song, "Call Me Flo," in *A Winsome Widow*, starring the Dolly Sisters in 1912, marked Kern's first association with Florenz Ziegfeld, the fabulous showman who glorified the American show girl and the American revue. Kern would soon be writing songs for the *Ziegfeld Follies*, and in the

1920's he would make stage history with Ziegfeld and *Show Boat*.

No less significant for Kern at this time was his first opportunity to write a complete stage score. This was for a Shubert production, *The Red Petticoat*—presented at Daly's theater on November 13, 1912—an unconventional musical adapted by Rida Johnson Young from her own nonmusical farce seen on Broadway one season earlier. Described as an "operetta *Girl of the Golden West*," this musical had for its setting Nevada, and for many of its characters miners. Grace Field was starred as a lady barber; Helen Lowell provided comedy as a voluptuous, somewhat vulgar, old maid in search of love. Their performances had much to recommend them, but due to a ponderous and static book the novel situations did not quite come off. *The Red Petticoat* was a failure. One Kern number had particular interest: "Since the Days of Grandmama."

Before Kern achieved his first substantial Broadway success he wrote a complete score for a second musical, *Oh, I Say*, presented in 1913. An interesting musical feature of this production was the effective use of saxophones in the orchestra at a time when the saxophone had not yet begun to dominate popular musical scoring.

Kern also interpolated songs in about half a dozen plays. Then on August 24, 1914, *The Girl from Utah*, Kern's first New York stage success, came to the Knickerbocker theater. Actually *The Girl from Utah* cannot be regarded as an intrinsically Jerome Kern musical, although it is sometimes designated as such. It originated in London with a score by Paul Rubens and Sidney Jones and a cast headed by Ina Claire in the title role. Transferred to Broadway, *The Girl from Utah* was revised to embrace eight new songs by Kern and boasted an American cast with Julia Sanderson, Donald Brian, and Joseph Cawthorn.

Julia Sanderson was "the girl from Utah" who fled to London to avoid becoming one of several wives of a Utah Mormon. Joseph Cawthorn and Donald Brian, respectively cast as Trimpel and Sandy Blair, are her London allies in her frenetic attempt to elude the pursuing Mormon, and to bring to fruition her rapidly flowering romance with Sandy.

Of Kern's eight songs, one added buoyancy and gaiety to the proceedings, a jaunty rhythmic number called "Why Don't They Dance the Polka Anymore?" A second touched the production with sentiment, the tender and nostalgic melody, "I'd Like to Wander With Alice in Wonderland." A third lifted *The Girl from Utah* both to significance and success, for it was the first in which Kern's personal creative identity was finally established: "They Didn't Believe Me."

The lyric of "They Didn't Believe Me" was written by Herbert Reynolds with the hope that when Kern had set it to music it could be sold to Al Jolson. With his sure instincts Kern preferred making the song into a haunting ballad for a voice and personality like that of Julia Sanderson, whose poignant projection was no minor influence in swelling the triumph of the song into a two-million copy sheet music sale. The way in which the melody of the refrain expands opulently for eight bars in simple quarter notes (with the line beginning "your lips, your eyes, your cheeks, your hair"), the way a poignant climax is achieved through a subtle change of key—this is sheer Jerome Kern magic. Equally remarkable is the way in which, in the recapitulation of the opening section, Kern suddenly introduces a new four-bar thought before proceeding with his original intentions. Freshness was further injected into the melody with an immediate change of rhythm from consecutive quarter and half notes to triplets in the much discussed and criticized phrase "and I'm certainly going to tell them." In the New York *Tribune*, F. Brock Pemberton was particularly critical of the banality of this verbal digression in the lyric. But if this is a fault, the fault is Kern's not Reynold's. It was Kern who suggested the insertion of this phrase to permit him greater rhythmic elasticity.

Victor Herbert heard the score of *The Girl from Utah* when it was first completed: Max Dreyfus had Kern play it for Herbert at the Harms office. "This man," Herbert told Dreyfus, "will inherit my mantle." In the next few years Kern and Herbert established an informal musical relationship by freely interpolating their songs into each other's productions.

The moment has come to puncture another Kern fable. There is hardly a biographical story about Kern (including his screen biography, *Till the Clouds Roll By*) which does not dramatize a fateful episode supposed to have happened to Kern in 1915. The incident concerned a projected trip Kern planned to take to England with Charles Frohman. A clock set by Kern to awaken him well in time for the sailing (so goes the story long accepted as fact) failed to go off. Kern overslept and missed the sailing. The boat he missed was the *Lusitania*, torpedoed by a German submarine ten miles off the coast of Ireland on May 7, 1915, claiming 1,198 lives including that of Frohman. But those who were closest to Kern at the time, including his wife, insist that this story simply has no basis in fact. Kern had no plans whatsoever to go to England with Frohman, and never intended sailing on the *Lusitania*.

7

"The Opening Chorus of an Epoch"

In 1914 Elizabeth Marbury—agent, producer, and, with F. Ray Comstock, comanager of the Princess theater in New York—planned to bring in from London, *Mr. Popple of Ippleton,* a Paul Rubens operetta. At her apartment she introduced one of her younger writing clients, Guy Bolton, to Kern; she wanted them to form a collaboration to adapt the text and the music of this English production for American consumption.

Guy Bolton was twenty-eight. Of English birth and the son of a famous engineer, he had been trained as an architect, a calling he followed in the United States where he helped design the Soldiers and Sailors Monument in New York. But he wanted to be a writer. By 1914 he had published several stories and sketches in *The Smart Set,* and had written two produced Broadway plays.

When Bolton and Kern first started working together it

"*The Opening Chorus of an Epoch*"   55

was not on *Mr. Popple of Ippleton*. As Bolton disclosed to this writer in a personal communication:

> After I met Jerry up at Bessie Marbury's, he came to me and said he had been asked to write a musical for Marie Cahill, and would I like to do the book. We neither of us discerned that Marie was on her way out. She and May Irwin and, I suppose Lillian Russell, were all very much of the same vintage, and also figure. Anyhow I did see that the job called for writing for a pretty mature actress and I remembered that Bernard Shaw had written *Captain Brassbound's Conversion* for Ellen Terry when she was about the same age. I therefore wrote a similar type of story with a bad man played by Pedro de Cordaba, and a comedy part for Richard Carle that was too strong to please his costar. Marie's husband, Dan Arthur, was the manager. The play was called *90 in the Shade* and it opened, if my memory serves, in Long Branch.

In its final state, *90 in the Shade*—which came to the Knickerbocker theater on January 15, 1915—concerned a rich American widow in the Philippines who, discouraged by the many amatory diversions of her betrothed, finally finds love with the captain of a smuggling vessel. There was some refreshing gaiety in the way this charming woman seeks to tame a primitive man. And two Kern numbers in a score entirely his were of some delight: "Whistling Dan" and "Where's the Girl For Me?". But *90 in the Shade* was a failure, suffering mainly from the fact that its star was now long past her prime.

Only after *90 in the Shade* had been put out of the way did Bolton and Kern get down to work on *Mr. Popple of Ippleton*. They were asked to make only the most necessary changes and to keep these down to a minimum. When their version was first tried out in New York at a private charity performance most of the audience started walking out during the first act. Elizabeth Marbury now decided to give Kern and Bolton a freer hand in making revisions. Bolton was paid a flat fee of five hundred dollars for this job, while Kern in deference to his now established position and reputation was engaged on a royalty basis. Certain significant production limitations, however, were set for them. One of the reasons why Marbury wanted to produce this play was to provide a tenant for her Princess theater, which had been suffering serious financial reverses. This theater was one of the smallest in New York, accommodating only about three hundred; it was almost impossible to find enough shows to play in so small a house. Marbury consequently conceived the idea of preparing productions specifically for this miniature auditorium—productions both economical and intimate, calling for a budget not in excess of $7,500. Everything had to be conceived along a modest design. The number employed in the cast and in the orchestra had to be limited, while the sets and costuming were to be few and modest. *Mr. Popple of Ippleton* was planned as a midget musical.

Bolton and Kern entirely rewrote that musical, renamed it *Nobody Home*, and brought it to the Princess theater on April 20, 1915. *Nobody Home* proved to be the first of an historical series of musicals henceforth identified as the "Princess Theater Shows," with which a new genre was introduced in the American musical theater, one which finally revolutionized long accepted procedures and remedied long tolerated abuses.

One of the principal abuses suffered by the American musical stage at this time was in the subservience of significant elements of good theater to spectacular sets, costumes, and stage effects. From the time of *The Black Crook* in 1866 —with its lavish ballets, transformations, and breathtaking scenic tricks—the first consideration of many Broadway producers of musicals was to electrify audiences with mammoth stage forces, opulent visual displays, Gargantuan production numbers, and stunning stage manipulations. The play, the music, the dance, the humor, at times even the star performers were incidental—just the convenient hooks on which to hang some eyefilling routine or some spectacular episode. In the 1910's this fetish for bigness and garish display was being catered to at the Hippodrome theater with annual extravaganzas or spectacles; the first, *A Society Circus*, presented in 1905. No less prodigal in production procedures was the *Follies* which Florenz Ziegfeld had been producing each year since 1907, or the *Passing Shows* put on by the Shuberts from 1912 on. Since the turn of the century most successful operettas were also mounted extravagantly: *The Wizard of Oz, Babes in Toyland, The Prince of Pilsen, Fantana, Madame Sherry, The Pink Lady,* and *Chin-Chin.*

Operetta had been dominating the American theater ever since the Gilbert and Sullivan comic opera *H.M.S. Pinafore* had enjoyed such an unprecedented triumph in 1878. In the ensuing two decades a vogue set in for the opéra-bouffe, operettas, and comic operas of Offenbach, Von Suppé, Johann Strauss, and Gilbert and Sullivan; and in the 1900's and 1910's for the pleasing English operettas of Ivan Caryll, Lionel Monckton, Leslie Stuart, Sidney Jones, and Paul Rubens. When American composers and librettists started writing operettas of their own they inevitably followed the approaches of, and reached for the standards established by, their European colleagues; there was little essentially American in either the text or the music of Willard Spencer's *The Little Tycoon* in 1887, Reginald De Koven's *Robin Hood* in 1890, Woolson Morse's *Wang* in 1891, and William Wallace Furst's *The Isle of Champagne* in 1892. The texts exploited foreign or exotic settings against which handsomely costumed characters moved within formula-ridden love complications.

As Guy Bolton once described these stilted operetta plots: "A prince from some neoBalkan country, disguised, is in love with a poor maiden. She does not know he is a prince; he does not know she is the daughter of an Albanian Croesus. . . . There is one situation in every act; the rest is gaps. Comedians filled these gaps—with gun scenes, timetable scenes, soda-fountain scenes."

The music imitated either the three-quarters time writing of the Austrians and Germans, or the well-mannered, neatly proportioned and distinctly Continental lyricism of the English operetta masters. What matter if the plot was hackneyed? What if the denouement lacked plausibility, the characters were stereotypes, the humor proved synthetic, and the situations were painfully contrived? What did matter a great deal was that the tunes were light and gay, the settings and costumes colorful, and the dance and production numbers lavish.

Thus the Princess Theater Shows represented for Broadway a radical departure in stage esthetics. As Guy Bolton explained in the New York *Dramatic Mirror:*

> [The Princess Theater Show was] straight, consistent comedy with the addition of music. Every song and lyric contributed to the action. The humor was based on the situation, not interjected by comedians. . . . Realism and Americanism were other distinguishing traits. . . . Americans laugh more naturally at a funny hotel clerk or janitor than at a crudely drawn cannibal princess.

The Princess Theater Show usually consisted only of two simple sets and a handful of characters. When chorus girls were required (and they were sometimes dispensed with entirely) they were about eight in number, each dressed in her individual costume. The orchestra boasted about ten instrumentalists.

Since the Princess Theater Show could not afford to pay the salary demanded by stars, it had to aim for well-balanced casts where the interest was evenly distributed among several characters. Unable to command the price for large casts or elaborate stage mechanics and settings the Princess Theater Show had to concentrate on witty dialogue, unusual plot twists, and fresh, and at times novel, American backgrounds, situations, and characters. Music, dance, humor were well integrated with the other elements of the production. By accomplishing all this the Princess Theater Show helped to explore a new world for the American musical theater.

Nobody Home was intimate and charming, studded with bright lines, filled with amusing episodes. It presented an amusing caricature of an Englishman who gets involved with an American show girl in New York. The music for eleven instruments, freshly and imaginatively scored by Frank Sadler, included two remarkable songs by Kern: "The Magic Melody" and "You Know and I Know." So prominently did a song like the "The Magic Melody" stand out from other music then being written for the Broadway stage—not merely for its sensitive lyricism but also for its striking modulations—that one of America's leading musicologists, Carl Engel, was led to write:

> Unless I am very much mistaken, "The Magic Melody" by Mr. Jerome Kern was the opening chorus of an epoch. . . . A young man gifted with musical talent and unusual courage has dared to introduce into his tune a modulation which has nothing extraordinary in itself, but which marked

a change, a new regime in American popular music. It was just the thing that the popular composer in the making had been warned against by the wise ones as a thing too highbrow for the public to accept. They were the foolish prophets. The public not only liked it; but they went mad over it. And well they might be for it was a relief, a liberation.

The hundred and more performances enjoyed by *Nobody Home* convinced Elizabeth Marbury of the validity of her innovation and gave her the momentum to proceed along similar lines. On December 23, at the Princess theater, she produced *Very Good, Eddie*, once again with a text by Guy Bolton and music by Kern. *Very Good, Eddie* ran for over a year, was hailed by the critics, and paid off a profit in excess of $100,000. The Princess Theater Show was now an institution on Broadway.

Very Good, Eddie (title derived from a catch phrase popularized by Fred Stone in one of his extravaganzas) was a delightful comedy of marital errors adapted from *Over Night*, a stage farce by Philip Bartholomae. Two honeymoon couples about to board a Hudson River Day Line boat get disentangled; the bride of one couple finds herself aboard ship with the groom of the other. For the sake of appearances they are compelled to maintain a fiction that they are married to each other, with often embarrassing and hilarious consequences. Ernest Truex and Alice Dovey portrayed this hapless couple with a deft touch that lifted many of the suggestive lines and situations above vulgarity to sophistication.

> With little or no space separating the players from the audience, [wrote Cecil Smith in his book, *Musical Comedy in America*,] *Very Good, Eddie* depended upon the ease and credibility of the acting and characterization. Scarcely any previous musical comedy had been favored with a plot and

dialogue so coherent, so neatly related to those of well-written musical plays.... A few critics spoiled by the louder and gaudier displays to which they were conditioned, cast aspersive phrases at *Very Good, Eddie* for its "kitchenette production," and another characterized it as "pleasing parlor entertainment that has found its way to the stage." But the body of playgoers found its principles acceptable and the intimate musical comedy became established as a suitable and successful genre.

Kern's music (lyrics by Schuyler Greene) often caught the ebullient spirit of the text—especially in a comedy gem delightfully presented by Ernest Truex in a rasping vocal style, "When You Wear a Thirteen Collar." But Kern had not abandoned his rare gift for beguiling lyricism, as was proved by "Nodding Roses" and "Babes in the Wood." One other point about Kern's score for *Very Good, Eddie* is worth remarking. For the first time—a practice Kern would pursue occasionally in later musicals, in one form or another—he subtly interpolated material from the world of classical music to remind his listeners that he was no unschooled Tin Pan Alley mechanic. In a delicate obbligato passage for celesta to one of his waltz tunes, Kern interposed a recognizable phrase from the then comparatively new opera by Richard Strauss, *Der Rosenkavalier*.

Among those who attended the opening night performance of *Very Good, Eddie* was Kern's one-time collaborator in London, P. G. Wodehouse. Wodehouse was paying his third visit to the United States, and serving as the drama critic of *Vanity Fair*. At the theater Kern suggested to Wodehouse that they revive their writing partnership. Later that evening Wodehouse joined Guy Bolton at Kern's apartment for a supper party with several other of Kern's friends, including Lawrence Grossmith, Vernon and Irene Castle, and Fay

Compton. As Kern accompanied Fay Compton in some of the songs from *Very Good, Eddie,* Wodehouse and Bolton huddled in a corner discussing ways and means of collaboration on the next Princess theater production. Each confided to his diary a version of how they finally got together on the project. Wodehouse wrote: "Went to the opening of *Very Good, Eddie.* Enjoyed it in spite of lamentable lyrics. Bolton, evidently conscious of this weakness, offered partnership. Tried to hold back and weigh suggestion, but his eagerness so pathetic that I consented."

Bolton's somewhat different version follows: "To Kerns for supper. Talked with P. G. Wodehouse, apparently known as Plum. Never heard of him, but Jerry says he writes lyrics, so being slightly tight, suggested we team up. Wodehouse was so overcome, he couldn't answer for a minute, then grabbed my hand and stammered out his thanks."

This decision to collaborate (however it may have been arrived at) had happy consequences. The Princess Theater Show acquired a third writing partner who could gracefully enter into the spirit of the venture. Wodehouse's sparkling lyrics were years ahead of their time in their wit, in the skill of the versification, in the simplicity of the prosody without descending to the ingenuous, in the avoidance of the trite and the stilted, and in the subtlety of phrase making. Later masters of the popular song lyric, including Lorenz Hart and Ira Gershwin, often expressed their indebtedness to and appreciation of Wodehouse. Those Wodehouse lyrics made such a bountiful contribution to the sophistication and merriment of the Princess Theater Shows that one unidentified critic was tempted to express his enthusiasm in the following verse:

> This is the trio of musical fame:
> Bolton and Wodehouse and Kern;

> Better than anyone else you can name.
>   Bolton and Wodehouse and Kern.
> Nobody knows what on earth they've been bitten by
> All I can say is I mean to get lit an' buy
> Orchestra seats for the next one that's written by
>   Bolton and Wodehouse and Kern.

But the first collaboration by Bolton, Wodehouse, and Kern was not a Princess Theater Show, but a more formal production: *Have a Heart*, a comedy about divorce, produced by Henry W. Savage on January 11, 1917. Although here could be found a more successful marriage of lyrics, text, and music than generally encountered on Broadway at the time—and although the production boasted an excellent performance by Billy B. Van and an equally outstanding comedy song in "Napoleon"—*Have a Heart* was a failure.

But their first Princess Theater Show, *Oh Boy!*, told quite another story. Opening one month after *Have a Heart*—on February 20—it achieved an even greater success than *Very Good, Eddie* had done, by running 463 performances. This time the text, entirely Bolton's, had an American college town as its setting. Tom Powers and Anna Wheaton were starred in a merry boudoir escapade in which a young lady must be secreted in the hero's apartment and assume various disguises and impersonations to escape discovery by the police and the hero's bride and relatives. Once again, as in *Very Good, Eddie*, Kern's nimble pen leaped with agility from humor to sentiment, always with a freshness of melodic invention. The humor was found in a sprightly take-off on the Mellor Gifford and Trevor song hit of 1912, "When It's Apple Blossom Time in Normandy," but with Flatbush, Brooklyn, as its locale and with the title of "Nesting Time in Flatbush." The sentiment appeared in one of Kern's most celebrated ballads, "Till the Clouds Roll By," a title used many years later for Kern's screen biography.

Oh Boy! was followed by another box-office bonanza—*Oh Lady, Lady* (a phrase made popular by Bert Williams). Besides its extended run at the Princess theater, where it arrived on February 1, 1918, *Oh Lady, Lady* for a time enjoyed a second company simultaneously at the Casino theater, and on one occasion was also put on at Sing Sing with an all-convict cast.

> Well, Bolton and Wodehouse have done it again, [wrote Dorothy Parker in a review]. If you ask me I will look you fearlessly in the eye and tell you in low, throbbing tones that it has it over any other musical comedy in town. . . . I like the way the action slides casually into the songs. I like the deft rhyming of the song that is always sung in the last act by the two comedians and the comedienne. And oh, how I do like Jerome Kern's music!

Wodehouse liked the plot of *Oh Lady, Lady* so well that several years later he used it for his novel, *The Small Bachelor*. It revolved around the embarrassment of a Long Island playboy, who on the eve of his wedding is confronted by his old girl friend. The gentleman's valet, a reformed crook, and the valet's wife, an experienced shoplifter, are additional succulent ingredients in a pungent stew for which the title song, and "Before I Met You," and "You Found Me and I Found You" was the gravy. *Oh Lady, Lady* might even have boasted a Jerome Kern song classic. "Bill"—which became famous in *Show Boat* a decade later—was written by Wodehouse and Kern for this play but was deleted when found unsuitable for Vivienne Segal, who played the part of Mollie Farringham, the playboy's old girl friend.

While *Oh Lady, Lady* was the last Princess Theater Show by Bolton, Wodehouse, and Kern it was not the last such show to be produced. Later the same year (1918) *Oh My Dear!* brought this epoch-making cycle of musicals to an end, this one with music by Louis Hirsch.

But the impact of the Princess Theater Shows on the American theater had already proved decisive. Out of the style, techniques, approaches, and nuances crystallized by the Princess Theater Show came the delightful intimate revues of the 1920's beginning with the *Grand Street Follies* and *The Garrick Gaieties*. The unconventional musical comedies of Rodgers and Hart—with their frequent excursions into satire and their adventurous avoidance of accepted traditions—undoubtedly also owed a large debt to the midget musicals that had preceded them.

Kern's part in this revolution can hardly be overestimated.

I have never felt, [wrote Richard Rodgers] that enough has been said of Kern's contribution to American music through his influence on subsequent writers of music in this country. . . . [As] the composer of the fabulous theater combination that contributed a form known as the Princess Theater Show . . . he was typical of what was and still is good in our general maturity in this country in that he had his musical roots in the fertile middle-European and English school of operetta writing and amalgamated it with everything that was fresh in the American scene to give us something wonderfully new and clear in music writing in the world. Actually, he was a giant with one foot in Europe and the other in America.

8

Grand Seigneur of Bronxville

In 1916 Jerome and Eva Kern rented a house on Sagamore Road in the New York suburb of Bronxville. Two years later they purchased their own house in the nearby Cedar Knolls section of Bronxville—a new three-floor multiroomed estate (quixotically named by Kern "The Nuts"), attended by several servants and a gardener. This was Kern's home for almost two decades. Through the years Kern continually kept adding more rooms to his sprawling, bulging house, together with all kinds of livestock to his property. For one period he owned several sheep, probably in a nostalgic effort to recreate an English setting, perhaps because he loved the sight of sheep grazing in the grass. He was finally forced to sell them because their wails during the night almost drove him mad. He had horses for himself and Eva: Eva's was a gift from Kern when she admired one of the lead ponies at the races; Kern's was purchased soon after that as a companion for Eva's horse. As household pets he owned various dogs and cats. He was particularly partial to a Boston terrier, Henry. When this dog once accidentally fell into a pool of water Kern did not hesitate to jump in, fully clothed though he was, to rescue it.

He continually kept adding to his possessions. He acquired his first car, an Overland, in 1916, and grew silently furious when Eva learned how to drive before he did. But he soon managed to learn, and initially was almost as proud of this accomplishment as of the writing of an outstanding song. He had no sooner learned to drive when, impulsively, he jumped into his car late one night, drove to P. G. Wodehouse's place, and dragged him from his bed to subject him to several hours of daredevil driving through the black countryside. Guy Bolton recalls other occasions in Bronxville soon after Kern had mastered the wheel when "in the middle of the night his puckish fancy would frequently take us off on all-night drives—to arrive surprisingly on the doorstep of some friend in the early hours of the morning. Once, when our welcome seemed a bit forced, Jerry insisted on getting back in the car, announcing that he had only dropped in for a five-minute chat." As it turned out the novelty of driving soon wore off completely and Kern gave it up. When in 1923 he acquired a Rolls Royce, he engaged a chauffeur who did all the driving. Later on, both in Bronxville and Beverly Hills, whenever Kern wanted to get anywhere he preferred to hire a chauffeur-driven automobile and leave his own cars in the garage.

Kern's partiality to elegant living led him in the 1920's not only to acquire the Rolls Royce, but also a speedboat for cruises on Long Island Sound; and after that a houseboat on which he traveled to Palm Beach and which, in 1930 and 1931, he used as auxiliary living quarters.

Within a convenient radius lived some of Kern's closest

friends of the theater: Max Dreyfus, Guy Bolton, and P. G. Wodehouse, among others. They were frequent visitors to "The Nuts" and helped enliven the evenings and nights with gay conversation. Kern also liked to be surrounded by others who had no association with either music or the stage but of whom he was exceptionally fond throughout his life. There were his cousins Walter and Elsie Pollak, the former a stockbroker; Lee Hartman, a wool merchant, and his wife Maud, with whom many years earlier Kern had been in love; Major and Mrs. Nathan Newman; Kern's lawyer, Mark Holstein; Kern's business manager, William Kron. The Kerns rarely entertained at home with festive dinners and elaborate parties, partly because of Eva's diffidence as a woman and her discomfort as a hostess, but mainly because Kern himself greatly preferred a room filled with friends, smoke, and gay talk. Since he habitually hated going to bed these sessions often dragged on for half the night. There was, to be sure, music as well as wit—usually the score or the songs in which Kern at the moment was most deeply involved. On more than one occasion Walter Pollak, an adequate amateur violinist, would contribute a pleasing obbligato to Kern's piano playing. It was characteristic of Kern's graciousness as host that whenever Pollak visited him there invariably was a violin at hand for his use.

Between 1915 and 1918, the heyday of the Princess Theater Shows, Kern concerned himself also with other kinds of musical productions. Among those for which he wrote a complete score was *Leave It to Jane* in 1917, again in collaboration with Bolton and Wodehouse. This was an adaptation of a George Ade play satirizing college life in an American Midwestern town. An attractive college widow (enchantingly played by Edith Hallor) uses her sex appeal to keep the college fullback star from defecting to a rival college. One of Kern's best humorous songs is found in this play: "Cleopatterer," charmingly presented by Georgia O'Ramey in the part of a comic waitress. Among the memorable serious numbers were the title song and "The Siren's Song."

On May 25, 1959, *Leave It to Jane* was revived in an off-Broadway production at the Sheridan Square Playhouse. After almost half a century Guy Bolton's once gay book proved sadly weather-beaten; the lyrics of P. G. Wodehouse, much less so. But Kern's music remained as much a joy to the ear and senses as it had been when first heard. "Ever since I listened to them from the second balcony of the Longacre theater in, heaven help me, 1917," reported Richard Watts, Jr., "I have remembered the Kern score with delight, recalling five of the songs in particular. And, hearing them again last night, I was happy to find that, not only was the score as a whole as charming and freshly tuneful as memory has made it, but my quintet came off easily the best of a gloriously melodious lot. . . . *Leave It to Jane* must stand on its unforgettable melodies."

Other productions with complete Kern scores, often with lyrics and texts by writers other than Bolton and Wodehouse, were failures in varying degrees and proportions. These included *Cousin Lucy* (1915), *Miss Information* (1915), *Love o' Mike* (1917); and in 1918, *Toot, Toot, Rock-a-bye Baby*, and *Head Over Heels*.

The last of these was produced by the venerable and redoubtable Colonel Henry W. Savage, whose age almost equaled the combined years of Kern, Bolton, and Wodehouse. Savage—whose production of *Have a Heart* had been the play for which Bolton, Wodehouse, and Kern had first joined forces—suggested that they write for him a new musical, entirely set on a train. Bolton discreetly remarked that a train could hardly be a locale suitable for a musical. "We pointed out the limitations imposed on the dancing line which would have a train corridor to perform in and would have to make its exit into either the 'Men's' or 'Women's' at the end of the numbers." But the three writers succumbed when, as inducement, the Colonel invited them to work aboard his Florida-bound yacht. What they discovered only after the boat had set sail was that the wily producer was somewhat short on crewmen and counted on the three writers to help with the boat chores. As soon as this situation had become appallingly clear Kern firmly told the Colonel that he and his collaborators had no intention of serving as hired help; that, as a matter of fact, on reconsideration they had decided not to write the musical Savage had suggested. This resolution was strengthened when all three writers came down with a case of fish poisoning and had to be brought ashore at Lake Worth.

Besides working on his own scores Kern produced many songs interpolated into musicals by other composers. By 1916 he became associated for the first time with the *Ziegfeld Follies* when four songs were interpolated into a score by Louis Hirsch and Dave Stamper. In 1917 Kern's songs appeared in an Emmerich Kálmán operetta, *Miss Springtime;* and in a Victor Herbert musical comedy, *Miss 1917*.

Miss 1917 was, as a matter of fact, a veritable cornucopia of theatrical riches. The cast included Lew Fields, Van and Schenck, Irene Castle, Peggy Hopkins Joyce, Vivienne Segal, Ann Pennington, Marion Davies, and George White. Sets were by Joseph Urban, choreography by Adolph Bohm, and staging by Ned Wayburn. Ziegfeld was one of the producers, and its two composers (Victor Herbert and Jerome Kern) were among the best on Broadway. Yet

Miss 1917 was a dismal failure, hardly surviving a month.

If it is today remembered at all it is not because of any of its distinguished collaborators, but because its rehearsal pianist was a young unknown named George Gershwin. He had recently graduated from Tin Pan Alley where he had been employed as staff pianist and song plugger, and he had written and published a few undistinguished songs.

Kern's enthusiasm for Gershwin's talent dates from *Miss 1917* where he was repeatedly impressed by Gershwin's extraordinary pianism and his remarkable gift at improvisation and arrangement. The first time Kern heard Gershwin play the piano he became so excited that though he did not like his wife to come down to rehearsals he insisted that she accompany him the next day just to hear this remarkable young musician. A year after *Miss 1917* closed, Kern arranged that Gershwin be hired as rehearsal pianist for *Rock-a-bye Baby*. During its rehearsal period in New York and out-of-town tryouts, the casual relationship between Kern and Gershwin flowered into friendship. Kern generously offered to give Gershwin advice, help and criticism whenever the younger man was ready to write his first musical-comedy score. The fact that Gershwin failed to take advantage of this offer in 1919 with *La, La, Lucille* wounded Kern so deeply that for two years he would have nothing to do with Gershwin. But by 1921 they were friends again, Kern now so completely sold on Gershwin's genius that a year later he intended to hand over to Gershwin one or two contractual assignments in which he himself had no interest. Gershwin never did actually get these contracts, but Kern remained one of his staunchest advocates and warmest admirers—even though through the years Kern felt (more strongly than justifiably) that Gershwin should confine himself exclusively either to concert music or to popular music.

9

Betty

The most significant change in Kern's personal life after his marriage with Eva came on December 16, 1918, with the birth of his only child, Elizabeth Jane. The Kerns had been married more than eight years and had begun to despair of having a child when Betty came along. Kern was elated. From her birth on he flooded her with favors and adoration. As a child, Betty was his toy; as a young girl, his playmate; as a young lady, a precious possession to be proudly exhibited. When he took her with him to social engagements he seemed to be "wearing" her in the same jaunty way a well-dressed man wears a carnation in his lapel or brandishes a gilt-knobbed cane. He petted and spoiled her. He made all the mistakes ascribed to indulgent parents, and many others of his own. He hired a governess and private teachers for her until she was eight. After that, when she was sent to public school in Bronxville, he had a nurse accompany her, and dressed her up in the most exquisite imported dresses.

Kern's friends also did their best to spoil her. Dorothy Stone, youngest member of the remarkable musical-comedy

Stone family that included father Fred and mother Allene, would make miniature copies of her costumes for Betty. The actor Lawrence Grossmith and the musical-comedy writer Ann Caldwell would come to "The Nuts" with an armful of gifts for her, and Noel Coward and Alexander Woollcott pampered and petted her. Max Dreyfus, whom she calls "Uncle Max" to this day, was a second overindulgent father.

She became, as might be reasonably expected, a self-indulgent, self-willed little girl. She recalls with amusement how, when she was only four, she was severely reprimanded by Irving Berlin for her self-assurance in saying, "I know it" after Berlin had praised her for being "a very nice little girl." She also remembers her spoiled-girl petulance at Jed Harris because he treated her like a child, when in her twelfth year she thought she was madly in love with him. She was given to sulking moods when people denied her wishes or when she was not the center of attraction.

At that, both her childhood and her girlhood were not easy—in spite of a generous and doting father and a self-sacrificing mother. To this day Betty recalls the agonies she suffered at school because she was the only one brought there by a nurse, and because she dressed the way she did. But apparently even more disturbing to her were her father's often contradictory attitudes and demands. He might be deeply concerned over the progress she was making at school and the course of study she was pursuing, but he did not hesitate to interrupt her schooling to take her with him on trips to Europe or Palm Beach. Betty's education consequently was haphazard; she never earned any degrees, and her schooling ended completely when she was seventeen.

Kern was contradictory in other ways, too. As far back as Betty's memory can reach into the past she remembers him treating her as an adult, by taking her among adults and discussing problems with her in an adult fashion. Yet at the same time he insisted upon considering her a child long after she had outgrown childhood; for example, he demanded that she go about chaperoned until her eighteenth year. And if he spoiled her to excess by catering to her slightest wish or whim, however unreasonable, he could be almost brutal and autocratic in his candor on what he knew to be the most important ambition of her life: to enter upon a career in the theater. "You are intelligent," he told her firmly, "but you haven't an ounce of talent." And that was that.

Today, Betty is the happily married wife of the successful motion picture producer, Jack Cummings, whose credits include *Seven Brides for Seven Brothers, The Last Time I Saw Paris, The Blue Angel,* and *Can-Can.* She is the proud mother of Steve and Linda. But Betty did not arrive at emotional maturity and a harmonious adjustment to living without first experiencing and suffering severe growing pains and undergoing various acute disturbances.

Her love for her father was no less intense than his for her. She always looks back with a refulgent glow to the bond that had existed between them. But at the same time she does not hesitate to confess that her childhood and adolescence were difficult times for her. Considering the way she treasures her memories of her father and her close associations with him, it is not likely she would have had it otherwise if she could. She has an overwhelming regret that her father had not lived until 1947 to see her life finally acquire a harmonious pattern through a happy marriage, after two brief and unhappy marital episodes, the first in 1939 with Dick Green, and the second in 1942 with Artie Shaw; and that her father did not also live to see his granddaughter, Linda, whose personality is so much like his.

10

Interval Between Two Epochs

Between 1920 and 1926 Kern wrote music for eleven Broadway musicals and had songs interpolated in three others. In the productions of this six-year interval the fresh and informal approaches of the Princess Theater Shows had been left behind. Like most other successful musicals of the early 1920's, those by Kern adhered to long existing conventions and esthetics of the American musical stage; the sound values of good theater regarding plot construction, characterization, dialogue, atmosphere, and realism were still permitted to languish.

Sally in 1920—book by Guy Bolton, lyrics shared by B. G. De Sylva and Clifford Grey—might well be considered the apotheosis of the kind of musical in vogue at the time. As produced by Ziegfeld, and with costumes and settings by Joseph Urban, it was a sumptuous feast for the eye, a veritable phantasmagoria of flaming colors and lavish scenes, extravagant production numbers and dance routines. All this splendor was the frame for the personality of its star, Marilyn Miller. The weekly salary of $3,000 which she earned as a percentage of the gross (the first time Ziegfeld ever made such an arrangement with a star) was the highest ever given to a musical-comedy performer up to that time, testimony of the unique place Miller had acquired in the theater. The play itself was the usual hodgepodge of confused identities. Sally is a forlorn dishwasher at the *Elm Tree Inn* who poses as a Russian dancer at a Long Island party; and Connie, a waiter at the Inn, is really a Balkan grand duke. The plot followed an inexorable rags-to-riches formula so greatly favored by the musical stage of that period. Sally's invasion of the Long Island estate leads to a career as dancer which culminates with triumphant appearances at the *Ziegfeld Follies* and marriage with the wealthy Blair Farquar. All the major roles represented stock characters so long familiar in musical comedy that they have only to make an appearance without preliminary identification to be instantly recognized.

If none of these shortcomings loomed large it was mainly because Marilyn Miller was Sally. "Marilyn," as Guy Bolton and P. G. Wodehouse recalled many years later in their book, *Bring On the Girls*, "gave to the play a curious enchantment that no reproduction in other lands or other mediums ever captures." Petite, of a slightness of build to suggest the precious Marilyn Miller was, as John Mason Brown once so aptly described her, a "Degas figure turned American . . . a Titania of the jazz age." When she appeared on the stage it became incandescent as if a garish floodlight had suddenly been poured upon it. She was the cynosure who reduced everything else around her to unimportance. When she danced she was the essence of grace; the lightness of body and foot had the diaphanous quality of a Mendelssohn scherzo. She had only a small voice, yet its hypnotic effect was inescapable.

Sally was one of the peaks in her fabulous career which had begun when she was only five as a member of a performing team that included her mother and stepfather. For ten years after that she toured the Variety theaters of England and the United States in a song-and-dance act. When she was fifteen, while appearing at the Lotus Club in London, she was seen by Lee Shubert, who contracted her to come to the Winter Garden. She made a triumphant debut there in *The Passing Show of 1914* where her dance routine as an exquisite Dresden doll, her singing of "Omar Khayyám," and her deft impersonations of several famous stage personalities of the time placed her instantly among Broadway's most luminous stars of the stage. She continued appearing in Broadway productions for the next four seasons, mainly in *The Passing Shows*. Then Florenz Ziegfeld wooed her away from Shubert with a fantastic salary offer. He considered her not only one of the most radiant stage performers of his experience but also one of the most beautiful women he had ever seen. He built his *Follies of 1918* principally as a showcase for her, where she was seen in several sumptuous scenes. In one of these she descended a flight of stairs in regal majesty, dressed in a tightly fitting, clinging minstrel costume. She also appeared as a ballet dancer; and she sang several songs. She returned to the *Ziegfeld Follies* for the last time a year later to make a smash hit of Irving Berlin's "Mandy."

Ziegfeld's most ambitious stage conceptions now had to take his favorite star into account. When, therefore, Kern and Bolton first discussed with him the idea for *Sally*, Ziegfeld knew at once who must play the title role. At that time

Ziegfeld also had in mind doing two other musicals, one each for Leon Errol and Walter Catlett. He suddenly decided to amalgamate all three projects into a single super production. A part for Errol was easily found in the role of Connie, a one-time duke who, as a waiter, becomes Sally's ally and strategist. It did not take much rewriting of the Bolton text to introduce the comedy character part of Otis Hooper for Walter Catlett.

Sally had everything a musical comedy audience in 1920 sought in escapist theater. It made no pretense at subtlety, wearing its many attractions on its sleeve. It had belly laughs in the eccentric dancing of Leon Errol and the droll, dry-humored antics of Walter Catlett. It piled visual effect upon visual effect with extravagant prodigality. And it brought the magic of Marilyn Miller's personality. "Sally is Marilyn Miller," reported Louis R. Reid in the New York *Dramatic Mirror*. "Her performance is one of the daintiest things of this unusual season." To her, Kern assigned one of his most beautiful melodies, "Look for the Silver Lining," in which he caught some of the radiance and glow of the star for whom it was written. But the bountiful score also included other treasures in "Whip-poor-will," "Wild Rose," the title song, and "The Little Church Around the Corner," the last shared in the closing scene by Leon Errol and a six-foot-one beauty named Dolores.

Kern originally planned having Marilyn Miller sing "Bill," the song to Wodehouse lyrics which had been written for but deleted from *Oh Lady, Lady*. But early in the rehearsals it became evident that Miller's voice was too slight for it, and once again the song had to be dropped. A few years later "Bill" found the right play and the right singer. The play was *Show Boat*. And the singer was a girl named Helen

Morgan who, it is interesting to note, was an obscure, ignored, last-row chorus girl in *Sally*.

Several Kern musicals after *Sally* deserve comment for various points of interest. The main significance of *Good Morning, Dearie* (1921) was the song "Ka-lu-a"; and "Ka-lu-a" has greater legal than musical importance. In 1919 Fred Fisher published "Dardanella," a song making effective use of a recurring rhythmic pattern in the bass (a device subsequently popularized in boogie-woogie music). The phenomenal success of this number was due mainly to this intriguing rhythmic background. Fisher rushed to the courts to sue Kern for expropriating in "Ka-lu-a" a technique he now regarded as his personal property. The courts agreed with him, recognizing the fact that this rhythmic device was basic to the Kern song. It awarded the plaintiff the modest damages of $250. But it is more than probable that one of the reasons Kern lost the case was because of his uncontrolled temper and acidulous remarks as a witness, which prejudiced the court against him.

In several other Kern musicals of the 1920-1926 interval, the focus of attention was more upon the stars than upon the scores, though there is hardly a Kern play which does not have at least one rewarding musical experience. In *Hitchy-Koo of 1920*, a young singer made her stage debut in an inconsequential role and as Julia Sanderson's understudy: Grace Moore, soon to become a star in Irving Berlin's *Music Box Revue*, and after that one of the most striking personalities in the world of grand opera. Fred and Adele Astaire were the principal attractions in an otherwise unimpressive production in 1922, *The Bunch and Judy*. Fred Stone; his wife, Allene; and their seventeen-year-old daughter, Dorothy, dominated *Stepping Stones* in 1923, a modernization of the Little Red Ridinghood fairy tale, tailor-made for their respective gifts. As Roughette Hood, Dorothy danced, sang, and acted her way to stardom for the first time. *Sitting Pretty*, in 1924, starred Queenie Smith, who had stepped to musical-comedy fame only one year earlier. And in 1925 *Sunny* brought the limelight back on Marilyn Miller.

Sunny was an attempt by Charles Dillingham to duplicate the triumph Marilyn Miller had previously achieved for Ziegfeld with *Sally*. Dillingham interested Kern in doing the music; he then called on Otto Harbach to work out the text. For a long time not a single feasible idea occurred to Harbach. He was on his way downtown to tell the producer he was bowing out of the project when the sudden thought came to him to combine two of his unproduced plays. By the time he reached Dillingham's office he had the plot clearly in mind. Marilyn Miller would play the part of a circus bareback rider in England, in love with a brash young American. Everyone concerned with *Sunny*—producer, composer, and especially the star—were delighted with Harbach's outline. Now given a green signal, Harbach called upon Oscar Hammerstein II, with whom he had already worked successfully, to help him with the text and lyrics. Thus it was that Kern began working for the first time with two important writers for the stage, both of whom were destined to achieve distinction in the musical theater as Kern's collaborators.

Otto Harbach (originally Hauerbach) was now, at fifty-two, one of Broadway's most distinguished musical-comedy librettists. In 1925, the year of *Sunny*, he had no less than five productions running on Broadway, including George Gershwin's *Song of the Flame* and Vincent Youmans' *No,*

No Nanette. A native of Salt Lake City, he had come to New York in 1901 after having taught English and public speaking at Whitman College in Walla Walla, Washington. He entered Columbia University to get a doctorate, but both his money and his eyesight soon started to give out and he left the University to hold various jobs, including those of insurance agent, newspaper reporter, and advertising copywriter. As an employee of George Batton's advertising establishment he began, in 1902, to write texts to Karl Hoschna's music. But it was five years before he met success, with Hoschna's *Three Twins*. *Madame Sherry*, in 1910, also with Hoschna's music, made it possible for him to give up all outside activity for the theater. When Hoschna died in 1911 Harbach began an association with Rudolf Friml which lasted more than a decade, beginning with *The Firefly* in 1912 and culminating with *Rose Marie* in 1924.

In writing the book and lyrics of *Rose Marie*, Harbach had been assisted by young Oscar Hammerstein II. Hammerstein had studied law at Columbia, but his heritage had predestined him for the stage. His grandfather was the renowned opera impresario, Oscar Hammerstein; his father, William, was the manager of New York's leading vaudeville theater, the Victoria; his uncle, Arthur, was a prominent producer on Broadway. It was his uncle who gave him his first chance to work in the theater, as assistant manager and general handy man for an Arthur Hammerstein production. One year later, in 1920, Hammerstein wrote text and lyrics of his first musical comedy, *Always You;* and soon after that he had his first success in *Tickle Me*, music by Herbert Stothart. It was with the latter production that Hammerstein first started a writing relationship with Otto Harbach. With Harbach, Hammerstein achieved his first stage triumphs:

in 1923 with *Wildflower,* music by Vincent Youmans; a year after that, with Rudolf Friml's *Rose Marie.*

Harbach knew Kern casually in the 1914-1915 period when Kern's name first became known on Broadway. A half-dozen years later, when Harbach lived in Yonkers, Kern casually dropped in upon him while riding horseback from his nearby Bronxville home. That started a more friendly relationship during which they often exchanged visits and sometimes talked of working together. Hammerstein's personal association with Kern was of a more recent date. Their first meeting took place in May, 1924 when both attended the funeral of Victor Herbert. Soon after that, when Hammerstein had been brought by Harbach into the *Sunny* project, he and Harbach visited Kern in Bronxville.

> I had been told Kern was a hard man to get along with, a tough guy, [was Hammerstein's reaction]. He certainly didn't seem so at first meeting. A man . . . with keen eyes and a quick smile, he bounced nimbly from one subject to another giving me the feeling that I would have to be very alert to keep pace with him. He and Otto and I discussed a plot they had already hit upon before my entrance into the collaboration. Jerry stuck to the high spots of the show. He didn't care what came in between. Otto and I could worry about that. He wanted to talk only about the big stuff and his talk developed it and made it bigger. He didn't play any music. It was all story and showmanship that day. But there were interludes when we didn't talk show. We skimmed over other topics and it seemed that Jerry knew something about everything. I felt stimulated and a little dazzled by him as I left his home that afternoon.

Sunny was contrived and pieced together like some giant jigsaw puzzle, to allow many different and at times irrelevant pieces to fit into the picture. Oscar Hammerstein II tells the story in the *Jerome Kern Song Book,* providing a

Jerome Kern: a camera study by Walter Pollak (1933)

Kern's mother and father, Fanny Kakeles Kern and Henry Kern

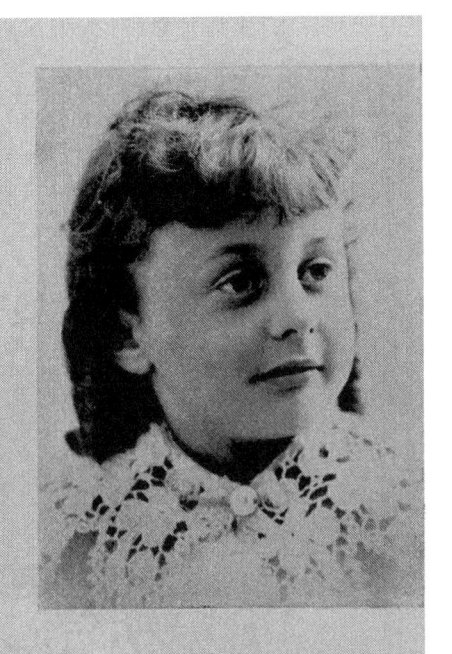

Kern at ages 4 and 15

Kern's first opus, 1902

Kern's wife, Eva, and daughter, Betty

Betty in reproduction of costumes from
Sally and *Sunny*—gifts of Marilyn Miller

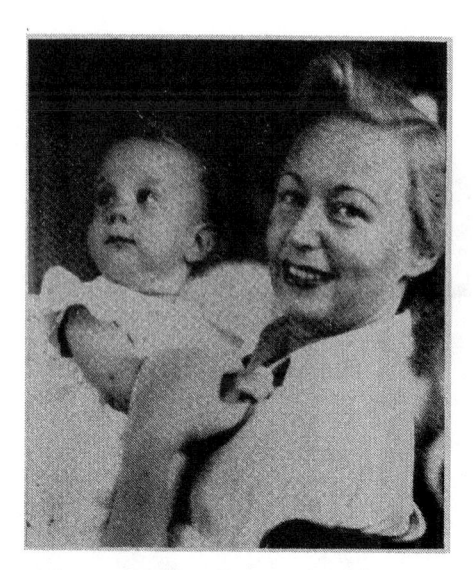

Betty Kern Cummings with
daughter, Linda, 1953

Last picture of Jerome Kern (with Betty), 1945

Across five generations: Kern beneath portrait of his grandfather, grandson, Steven, in his arms

Photographic study of Eva, Betty, and Jerome Kern by George Gershwin, 1937

Kern and His Collaborators

Guy Bolton (1920) *Francis Bruguiere*

P. G. Wodehouse *Blackstone Studios*

Bert Longworth, First National Studios

Otto Harbach, with straw hat, and Kern
on the set of First National Studios

Kern and Ira Gershwin (1943)

Photo by St. Hilaire, Columbia Pictures

Kern and Oscar Hammerstein II

Culver Service

Helen Morgan sings "Bill" in *Show Boat*

World's Fair scene from *Show Boat*

Vandamm Studio

Walter Slezak as the schoolmaster
in *Music in the Air*

Vandamm Studio

Ensemble from *Music in the Air*

Marilyn Miller in *Sally*

Lyda Roberti, Ray Middleton, and Bob Hope in *Roberta*

Robert Walker as Jerome Kern
in *Till the Clouds Roll By*

Cornell Wilde, Linda Darnell, and William Eythe in a scene
from the 20th Century-Fox production *Centennial Summer*

Walter G. Pollak
Kern and Myrna Loy

George Gershwin and Kern

Caricature of Kern drawn by
Arthur Kober during a poker game

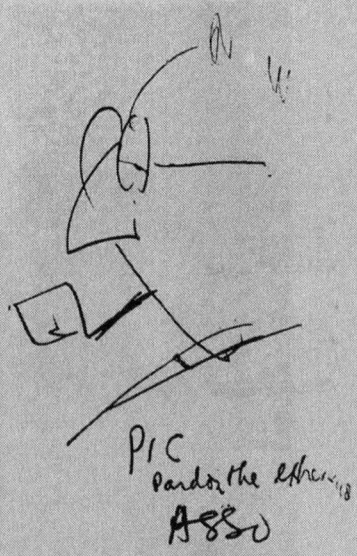

Portrait of Kern by George Gershwin

Camera study by Dick Green

Kern at Fisherman's Wharf, San Francisco, 1938

penetrating insight into the often functional and machine precision way in which a musical comedy was put together in those days.

> Our job was to tell a story with a cast that had been assembled as if for a revue. Charles Dillingham . . . had signed Cliff Edwards, who sang songs and played the ukulele and was known as Ukulele Ike. His contract required that he do his specialty between ten o'clock and ten-fifteen! So we had to construct our story in such a way that Ukulele Ike could come out and perform during the time and still not interfere with the continuity. In addition to Marilyn Miller, the star, there was Jack Donahue, a famous dancing comedian, and there were Clifton Webb and Mary Hay, who were a dance team of the time, Joseph Cawthorn, a star comedian, Esther Howard, another, Paul Frawley, the leading juvenile. In addition to the orchestra in the pit we also had to take care of George Olsen's band on the stage. . . . One episode stands out vividly in my memory. Before we went into rehearsal, Marilyn Miller returned from Europe and met us in Dillingham's office to listen to the story and score we had written so far. We went through the whole plot and described it, and sang whatever numbers we had written up to that point. She seemed to be listening very attentively. When we were all finished there was a pause, and then Marilyn said, "When do I do my tap specialty?"

For all that, *Sunny* was a major success, and in many ways a delight as well. Marilyn Miller was still able to surround everything around her with glamour, to bathe the stage with magic. And Kern's score produced one of the substantial hits of his career, and one of his standards, in "Who?". This number was so piquantly offered by Marilyn Miller in a duet with Paul Frawley that Kern was once tempted to say that she was that song's "editor, critic, handicapper, clocker, tout, and winner." Kern also never hesitated to concede that much of the credit for the huge commercial appeal of his song belonged to lyricists Harbach and Hammerstein. Kern had given them a tricky tune in which the melodic phrase of the refrain began with a single note sustained through two-and-a-quarter measures, or nine beats. Since a phrase could hardly be adapted for one sustained note, a single word was needed; but that one word had to carry such interest that it could be repeated five times in the refrain (with each return of the basic melodic phrase) without becoming monotonous. Kern, therefore, insisted that it was the use of the provocative—and highly singable—word "who" that had spelled the difference between failure and success.

11

"Warmth, Enchantment, Laughter, Music"

Edna Ferber first heard about show boats from the Broadway producer, Winthrop Ames. They were in New London, Connecticut, for the out-of-town tryouts of the George S. Kaufman-Edna Ferber play, *Minick*, when Ames—oppressed by production problems—remarked how wonderful it would be if they could forget all about Broadway and become a show-boat troupe. Since Ferber knew nothing about show boats he described to her how they used to drift the Southern rivers downstream, tie at a convenient landing, and give performances for audiences which had traveled many miles to see the show.

After *Minick* had opened in New York Edna Ferber did some digging of her own on the subject of show boats. The final outcome of this research was her novel, *Show Boat*, a best seller following its publication in 1926.

What first attracted Kern to Ferber's *Show Boat* was its title. He bought the book, read the first chapters, became enchanted by its background, and knew at once he would some day help to make it into a Broadway musical production. When Kern's musical comedy, *Criss Cross* (in which the Stone family was starred) opened on October 12, 1926, Kern approached Alexander Woollcott during intermission to ask Woollcott to introduce him to Edna Ferber. Only then did he learn that Edna Ferber actually was Woollcott's guest that evening, that at the moment she was hovering discreetly only a few yards away. Ferber recorded her first impression of Kern as follows: "A pixie little man with the most winning smile in the world, and partially eclipsed by large thick spectacles." Kern on his part was somewhat in awe of Ferber, whose novel *So Big* had won the Pulitzer Prize a year earlier. He soon came to the point. He wanted to acquire the musical-comedy rights to *Show Boat*. Thinking in terms of the musical theater as represented by *Criss Cross* and similar productions she had recently seen, Ferber was at first flabbergasted by this request. How could a musical comedy be made out of her novel? *Show Boat* with a chorus-girl line, tap dances, burlesque humor, stilted routines—impossible! Only after Kern had detailed that what he had in mind was not a conventional musical comedy but a musical play rich with American background, characters, and local color did she give her consent.

Once Ferber had been won over Kern proceeded to gain from Ziegfeld a verbal agreement that he would produce the show; also the interest of Oscar Hammerstein II in writing the libretto and lyrics.

From the first Kern and Hammerstein both decided that, to give their show boat smoother sailing, they would once and for all jettison the hackneyed conventions and practices of the traditional Broadway theater. Methods that had served them so well in piecing together a *Sunny*, for example, simply would not work for *Show Boat*, which could never be contrived for the convenience of stars and their specialties. The plot and situation could never be twisted and distorted out of shape to accommodate an eye winning piece of stage business. Much too long had the tail wagged the dog, and the cart pulled the horse! Now the first and basic consideration of the writers would be the play and the play alone. Everything else—song, dance, humor, costuming, sets, performers—would be subservient to the aesthetic and dramatic demands of the play, and not vice versa.

When Kern and Hammerstein started working each one prepared the outline of an adaptation, and later were delighted to discover that they were of a single mind regarding important details. They visited an old show boat in Maryland and attended one of its performances to gain local impressions. Every morning Kern would telephone Hammerstein—then living in Great Neck, Long Island—to play for him over the phone what he had worked out the previous day. They also spent many hours, usually at Kern's place in Bronxville, discussing characters, main scenes, and background, and how the songs would grow naturally from the play's structure.

"We had fallen hopelessly in love with it," Hammerstein explains. "We couldn't keep our hands off it. We acted out the scenes together and planned the actual direction. We sang to each other. We had ourselves swooning."

Ziegfeld had informed Kern and Hammerstein that he planned to open the new Ziegfeld Theater, then being built on Sixth Avenue and 53rd Street, with *Show Boat*. What neither Kern nor Hammerstein knew, however, was that Ziegfeld had made a similar promise to Guy Bolton and

Harry Tierney, then working on *Rio Rita*. By the time the theater was ready to open Kern and Hammerstein were still knee-deep in writing, but *Rio Rita* was ready, and it was with that production that the Ziegfeld Theater opened on February 2, 1927.

There might have been a great amount of exhilaration and stimulation for Kern and Hammerstein in the planning and writing of *Show Boat*. But during this period there were also many things to dampen their heady spirits, to fill them with foreboding. Just after *Rio Rita* opened in New York Kern became convinced that Ziegfeld was so broke after having sunk so much of his money into the erection of his sumptuous theater that Ziegfeld simply could not afford to produce *Show Boat*. With his customary directness Kern decided, one Sunday morning, to drive down with Hammerstein to Ziegfeld's place at Hastings-on-the-Hudson and ask the producer point-blank where he planned to get the money to produce their play.

> We drove into Ziegfeld's palatial grounds, and to an estate that resembled a European chateau, [Hammerstein now recalls with amusement]. There we were met by a butler who had the dignity of a banker and who ushered us into a magnificently furnished living room. A maid, dressed in exquisite lace and who herself might have just stepped out of some Ziegfeld production, conducted us to Ziegfeld's private quarters upstairs, through a regal bedroom, and into an immense bathroom in which the producer was being shaved by his personal barber. The shaving over, Ziegfeld put on his silk, brocaded dressing gown and invited us to have a "snack" with him. The "snack" consisted of a royal meal of roast beef and champagne with all the trimmings, attended by a retinue of butlers and waiters. By the time we left Ziegfeld late in the afternoon, not even Jerry had the brashness to ask him if he had any money.

But Ziegfeld kept postponing the date of production. First he wanted to take a long vacation, following the rigors of having put on *Rio Rita*. Back from that vacation he sought another prolonged postponement; *Rio Rita* was such a smash box-office success it simply was not feasible for Ziegfeld to take it off to make room for *Show Boat*. For a time Kern and Hammerstein seriously considered taking *Show Boat* away from Ziegfeld, especially since Arthur Hammerstein had expressed his eagerness for it. But when Arthur Hammerstein became too involved with another of Oscar's musicals, *Golden Dawn*, to give *Show Boat* immediate production, Kern and Hammerstein decided to string along with Ziegfeld after all, painful though this was proving to be. These delays nevertheless proved a blessing in disguise, as Hammerstein later conceded. Kern and Hammerstein were given more time in which to work and rework their play down to the smallest details. "That year's delay made *Show Boat* a much better play than it would have been had we produced its first draft."

"Ol' Man River" was one of several songs completed during this period of painstaking reappraisal and rewriting. Hammerstein felt the need for some musical number to convey to audiences the impact which the Mississippi River had had on the readers of Ferber's novel. He decided upon a character song to project the feel of the river. There was also a spot in the first act calling for a song without a situation. Hammerstein solved both problems with his simple, poignant paean to the Mississippi, that "ol' man river." "It is a song of resignation with a protest implied," Hammerstein explains, "sung by a character who is a rugged and untutored philosopher."

In her autobiography, *A Peculiar Treasure*, Edna Ferber

described her emotional response when she first heard "Ol' Man River."

> Jerome Kern appeared at my apartment late one afternoon with a strange look of quiet exaltation in his eyes. He sat down at the piano. . . . He played and sang "Ol' Man River." The music mounted, mounted, and I give you my word my hair stood on end, the tears came to my eyes, and I breathed like a heroine in a melodrama. This was great music. This was music that would outlast Jerome Kern's day and mine. I have never heard it since without the emotional surge.

Another important song, the duet of Magnolia and Ravenal, "Why Do I love You?", was written while the show was trying out in Washington, D.C., as a replacement for another song that did not fill the bill. "Why Do I Love You?", incidentally, was the means by which Hammerstein was able one day to feed Kern some of that brand of impishness for which the composer himself was so famous. Hammerstein knew, of course, that Kern had a horror of the word cupid in a song lyric. When Kern provided him in Washington with the new melody for the love duet Hammerstein retired to his suite at the Willard Hotel and finally emerged with a lyric that started with "cupid knows the way" and continued through a series of bromides and platitudes generously sprinkled throughout with the word cupid. Kern caught on, enjoyed the joke, but felt even better when Hammerstein then gave him the real lyric he had written for the melody. The bogus cupid lyric for a long time hung framed in Kern's study in Beverly Hills, but it is now in Hammerstein's possession.

If "Ol' Man River" and "Why Do I Love You?" came comparatively late in the writing of *Show Boat* a third of its song masterpieces, "Bill," preceded it by some fifteen years. As we have already remarked, this song, with lyrics by

P. G. Wodehouse, was originally intended for the Princess Theater Show, *Oh Lady, Lady*, where it was found unsuitable; after that a place was sought for it in *Sally*, but with no greater success. What suddenly made Kern reach in his well-stocked notebook for "Bill" while he was working on his *Show Boat* score was a dark, tousel-haired, dewy-eyed singer with a throbbing voice who had been cast as the half-caste Julie—Helen Morgan. Formerly a comptometer operator, biscuit packer, winner of a beauty contest, and chorus girl—more recently night-club performer and featured singer in the *George White Scandals* and *Americana*—Morgan had been discovered for *Show Boat* in the last-named revue in 1926. There she had brought down the house nightly in a sultry rendition of a blues song, "Nobody But Me," while seated atop an upright piano in the orchestra pit. "Bill" belonged so naturally both to Helen Morgan and to the character of Julie that Kern did not hesitate in this one instance to sidestep his avowed intention of having each song in *Show Boat* written expressly for the situation or character for which it was intended. And, following the practice first initiated in *Americana*, Kern had her sing "Bill" seated on an upright piano.

Since "Bill" was the only lyric in *Show Boat* not by Hammerstein, he has since often been erroneously designated as its author, despite his and Kern's persistent attempts to place the credit where it belonged. For the 1946 revival of *Show Boat* Hammerstein (on Kern's suggestion) inserted a special note in the program to set the record straight:

> I am particularly anxious to point out that the lyric for the song "Bill" was written by P. G. Wodehouse. Although he has always been given credit in the program, it has frequently been assumed that since I wrote all the other lyrics

for *Show Boat* I also wrote this one, and I have had praise for it which belonged to another man.

Placing Helen Morgan in the part of Julie was a happy bit of casting. Though she had never before appeared in any musical production other than a revue and though she had little acting technique, everything she did as Julie was, as Hammerstein says, "exactly right. Her instincts were sure. Nobody had to tell her how to move, gesture, or put over a song. She behaved like a veteran."

The rest of the casting was equally felicitous. Norma Terris and Howard Marsh were Magnolia and Gaylord Ravenal; Charles Winninger, Cap'n Andy; Jules Bledsoe (like Helen Morgan, a comparative newcomer), Joe; Edna May Oliver, Parthy Ann Hawks; Eva Puck and Sammy White, Ellie and Frank. Nobody was starred because though most were distinguished performers with rich stage careers behind them, none was actually of star caliber, no one was more important than the others. It was mainly through *Show Boat* that most of the leading performers subsequently became stars of first rank.

The casting was one reason why the initial production went off so well. Another was the fact that *Show Boat* lent itself to the fabulous Ziegfeld touch. The late nineteenth century American setting allowed for vivid, colorful costuming. The backgrounds of a show boat, an intimate auditorium within the boat, and the Chicago world's fair could give immense scope to a scenic designer's invention. Ziegfeld did not have to inhibit himself in his partiality toward elaborate visual display, and *Show Boat* did not have to suffer from such inhibitions. Joseph Urban and John Harkrider, who designed sets and costumes respectively, were given free rein to let their imaginations go and with breathtaking results.

Always a stickler for detail, Ziegfeld considered no element in the production unimportant; nothing on the stage escaped his dissecting eye. Such fastidious attention to small matters gave *Show Boat* its wonderful integration; but at times it also proved a trial to the writers. At one of the rehearsals Hammerstein slipped into a seat next to Ziegfeld to describe an important revision he was making in the second act. Ziegfeld did not hear a word. All the while he was noticing that one of the girls on the stage had that day changed her hairdo, and he was more interested in getting her to return to her earlier hairdressing than in hearing about Hammerstein's changes.

At the initial rehearsals Hammerstein not only read the parts of roles not yet cast, but also served as a director, since one had not yet been engaged. Always soft-spoken, unobtrusive, and reluctant to press his importance, Hammerstein was one day mistaken by Helen Morgan for an extra and she tried to use her still limited influence to get him hired for a part in the play. Hammerstein, incidentally, did so well in the direction (always aided by Kern) that a formal director was never actually hired.

Show Boat was conceived ambitiously along spacious designs. For it was a "big" show in every sense of the adjective, including the actual length of the play itself. When *Show Boat* went to the National Theater in Washington, D.C., to begin a two-week tryout on November 15, 1927, it was so long that though the curtain went up promptly at 8:15 it did not go down again until 12:30. All the rest of that night Kern and Hammerstein worked in their suites at the Willard Hotel trying to cut the production down to practical size.

Despite the fact that a matinée had been scheduled for the following day the cast was assembled for a morning rehearsal to incorporate the cuts in time for the afternoon performance. But that performance did not end before six. Another hour had to be sliced out of the play, which the collaborators felt consisted now entirely of essentials.

More deletions were made during the next few weeks as the production proceeded on to the Erlanger Theater in Philadelphia on December 5. Nevertheless, when *Show Boat* finally opened at the Ziegfeld in New York on December 27, it was still too long by half an hour. But if there was any sign of fatigue on the part of that first-night audience it was not reflected in their enthusiastic reaction. Nor was any fatigue found in the critics' appraisal the following morning. "A wonder and a wow . . . an American masterpiece which is never too precious for dancing, never too elegant for fun," was the way Robert Garland described it. "From any angle," said Stephen Rathbun, "*Show Boat* deserves the highest praise." "A complete demonstration of the composer's and lyric writer's dependence on their basic idea," noted Alison Smith; while Richard Watts, Jr. called it a "triumph, a beautiful example of musical comedy."

For all its departure from the norm *Show Boat* proved as successful at the box office as it was in the reviews. During its almost two years' run in New York it averaged a weekly gross of $50,000. After that it embarked on an equally successful national tour, beginning with a stay in Boston from May 6 to June 15, 1929, and continuing across the country from September, 1929, to March, 1930. The original company—with Paul Robeson replacing Jules Bledsoe as Joe, and Dennis King taking over from Howard Marsh the part of Ravenal—returned for a new New York run of 180 performances at the Casino Theater on May 19, 1932. *Show*

Boat was also produced in London at the Drury Lane on May 3, 1928, and soon after that in a French translation in Paris. In 1929 the first motion-picture adaptation was released: a Universal Picture starring Laura La Plante, Joseph Schildkraut, and Alma Rubens in what was only partly a talking picture, but with the songs and a synchronized musical score.

The instantaneous success of *Show Boat* wherever it was seen was proof that—shrewd showmen that they were—Kern and Hammerstein had not sacrificed entertainment value for bold, new concepts of musical theater. *Show Boat* was a rich, colorful, nostalgic chapter from the American past, filled with humor, gentle pathos, tenderness, and high drama. It bewitched the eye, ear, and heart; and it never offended the mind. It was a relevation; and it was a revolution. Here was something unique in the musical theater of that day: an American musical comedy with dramatic truth; a plot with a logical, believable line; a love story that rang true. The poignant tale of Magnolia and the river-boat gambler, Gaylord Ravenal—which carried them through marriage, separation after the birth of their daughter, Kim, and ultimate reconciliation on the show boat where first they met—struck a human note to which audiences could respond as if in reflex action. Here were three-dimensional characters in place of the cardboard images previously populating the musical stage—characters like Cap'n Andy and Parthy Ann Hawks to contribute humor to the play from the quirks and idiosyncrasies of their personalities rather than from synthetic situations or the artificial exchange of repartee carefully contrived by a librettist. Here was authenticity of background and atmosphere, whether on the levee of the Mississippi, aboard the show boat *Cotton Blossom*, at the Midway Plaisance of the Chicago world's fair, or at the

Trocadero Music Hall. Here were dialogue and lyrics that were supple, fresh, and imaginative—capable of soaring to poetic heights without abandoning the vernacular and the idiomatic. In *Show Boat*, Oscar Hammerstein II—up to now little more than a skillful technician and a functional writer —had suddenly discovered within himself new creative resources.

And, finally, here was a musical score which was an extravagant outpouring of the most wonderful melodies. Few American stage productions before or since boasted so many song hits that subsequently became popular classics: not merely the already mentioned "Ol' Man River," "Why Do I Love You?", and "Bill," but also "Only Make Believe," "Can't Help Lovin' That Man," and "You Are Love." Kern had previously demonstrated his melodic powers. In *Show Boat* he was still a master of melody, but his melody now had greater versatility, greater variety and range of mood and feeling. Kern now became the inspired composer of spirituals and blues as well as ballads and popular show tunes.

> This is a score, [wrote Olin Downes, music critic of the New York *Times*] which, by reason of its melodic inspiration, its workmanship, its reflection of period and environment, has . . . won the position of a classic of its kind. It was created by a singularly gifted man, who had mastered his business . . . and its success has been richly deserved.

12

A Footnote on Show Boat

A new art form emerged in the American musical theater with *Show Boat:* the musical play as distinguished from musical comedy. There have been many significant productions since 1927 to advance this form and establish it as one of America's major contributions to the theater of the world: the musical plays of Rodgers and Hammerstein, Kurt Weill, Leonard Bernstein, Frank Loesser, and Lerner and Loewe. Since *Show Boat* first drifted into harbor stage techniques have become increasingly slicker; dramatic approaches more subtle and sophisticated; musical values deeper, richer, and more operatic. But though it was one of the first of its kind, *Show Boat* still remains one of the best. It never fails to cast a spell on an audience.

Two decades after its original presentation *Show Boat* was given a new and revitalized production at the Ziegfeld Theater, on January 4, 1946. Kern and Hammerstein were the producers; Hassard Short did the staging; costumes

98   JEROME KERN

and sets were designed by Lucinda Ballard and Howard Bay; and the cast included Jan Clayton, Charles Fredericks, Kenneth Spencer, Ralph Dumke, and Carol Bruce. Only several minor changes had been made in the original version. One "front scene," three minor musical episodes, and Magnolia's imitations of the stars of the Twenties were omitted. In their place the dances were extended, choreography by Helen Tamiris and dance performances by Pearl Primus and her Negro troupe. A new song was interpolated for Kim in the last scene, "No One But Me" (the last song Kern was destined to write). But basically this was the same *Show Boat* that had enjoyed such an historic cruise in 1927-1928.

After a quarter of a century *Show Boat* was returning to a much-changed world. America had passed through and been changed by the social upheavals of the New Deal and the Roosevelt administrations. The entire world had felt the shattering impact of the depression and the rise of fascism, the second world war, and the harnessing of nuclear energy. Motion pictures had acquired a voice, the phonograph had achieved high fidelity, television had entered the home. The serious American theater had begun to tap new veins of poetry and imagination with such younger men as Tennessee Williams and William Saroyan, while the musical theater had been carried toward a new destiny with *Oklahoma!* by Rodgers and Hammerstein. When *Show Boat* returned to New York in 1946 three stars of the original production were dead (Helen Morgan, Edna May Oliver, and Jules Bledsoe), and so were Ziegfeld, Joseph Urban, and Kern himself. Norma Terris was now the wife of Ziegfeld's physician; Sammy White was divorced from his wife, Eva Puck; and Howard Marsh was operating a night club in New Jersey.

Yet, radically changed though both the world and the

theater in which *Show Boat* was born had become, the musical still proved so vital, fresh, and exciting to a new generation of theatergoers in 1946 that it gave over 400 performances in New York, was seen by 584,000 people there, and grossed over two million dollars. The play had lost none of its magic. It was still a "musical play in the grand manner . . . what every musical should be—and no other has been," as John Chapman said; a play still noteworthy for its "melodic magnificence, dramatic excitement and abiding humor," in the words of Howard Barnes.

Two years after that—an interval in which the 1946 production toured the country—the firm of Rodgers and Hammerstein brought *Show Boat* back to Broadway with several changes of cast. "Can't help loving that treasure house of melodies and legends," now exclaimed Brooks Atkinson.

Show Boat has become a classic of the American musical stage, a yardstick by which musicals are continually measured. In one version or another it is continually with us, and to our benefit. There is hardly a season when it is not being revived somewhere in the country, whether in a formal theater, an outdoor stadium, or a marine auditorium. In 1952 it was presented for the first time in a concert version, integrated and dramatized by a special narrative prepared by Hammerstein; at the Lewisohn Stadium in New York. On April 8, 1954, it received the highest tribute that can be paid to a Broadway musical by becoming the first such production to enter a regular opera repertory, that of the New York City Opera.

There have been two additional screen versions since the one in 1929. In 1936 Irene Dunne, Allan Jones, Paul Robeson, Helen Morgan, and Charles Winninger appeared in a now all-talking, singing Universal production that included two new Kern-Hammerstein songs, "I Have the Room Above

Her" and "Ah Still Suits Me." In 1951 Metro-Goldwyn-Mayer released a new screen version with Ava Gardner, Kathryn Grayson, Howard Keel, Joe E. Brown, and William Warfield.

The present day long-playing record catalogue lists over half a dozen different recordings of the *Show Boat* score, including one with the original cast of the 1946 stage revival, and another of the sound track of the 1950 motion picture. But there exists still another musical adaptation of the *Show Boat* music: a symphonic presentation of the principal melodies entitled *Scenario*, prepared by Kern himself. This was Kern's first excursion into the writing of orchestral music for the concert auditorium. It had been commissioned by the distinguished conductor of the Cleveland Orchestra, Artur Rodzinski, who felt this vital music deserved both a symphonic frame and the resources of a large symphony orchestra. Kern began working on this score early in July, 1941, and completed the orchestration in September. On October 23 Rodzinski gave the première performance with the Cleveland Orchestra, as the final number of a program that included major works by Beethoven, Paul Hindemith, and Mendelssohn. On November 19 Rodzinski directed the New York première at Carnegie Hall with the New York Philharmonic Orchestra.

The published score bears a dedication to Rodzinski and a quotation by Winston Churchill:

> The British Empire and the United States . . . together. . . . I do not view the process with misgiving. No one can stop it. Like the Mississippi, it just keeps rolling along. Let it roll . . . inexorable, irresistible, to broader lands and better days.

Scenario is by no means just a potpourri of familiar songs strung together through skillful modulations and transitions. Kern sought to write an integrated work: a symphonic portrait of the play itself; a transmutation in tones of the atmosphere, background, and dramatic content of both the novel and the play. A gentle passage in muted strings with which the work opens brings up the image of the Mississippi River. Four measures later the first horn appears with another subject suggesting the river. This is the motto material of the entire work, even as the Mississippi River itself is a subtle unifying element in the novel and the play. "Ol' Man River" is then used by the composer as a main theme; it is first heard softly in violas and bass clarinet, then given ample and at times passionate treatment, while the flute provides a discreet background with the music from the verse. This accompanying material from the verse is soon given some extended attention; so are such important melodies as "Only Make Believe," "Why Do I Love You?", and "Ol' Man River" in a final recall. In between these basic melodies from the play's score are skillfully interpolated snatches of melodies and themes suggesting calliope music, the vigorous accents with which roustabouts accompany their work of loading the Mississippi boats, Negro dance tunes, phrases of liturgical chants, realistic episodes depicting the crowds and the carnival scenes at the Midway of Chicago's world fair, and a fragment of barbaric African dance—all serving to inject more vivid local color to and to dramatize the atmospheric background of the composition.

13

End of an Epoch

To some of Kern's friends of the theater he appeared to have been strongly affected by the artistic acclaim of *Show Boat*. They feel Kern now began taking his music and himself much more seriously than heretofore; that though he was always saying he was not writing for posterity, he had begun to give more thought to the less temporal value of his work. These friends remark that the gift for laughter and gaiety which continually enlivened Kern's scores for the Princess Theater Shows was only passingly and infrequently encountered in his scores after *Show Boat*. Kern had now begun to search more and more for deeper content in his writing, for greater musical perspectives, for finer workmanship.

Be it as it may, *Show Boat* unquestionably gave Kern both the heightened strength and the growing curiosity to continue pursuing new paths in the theater. Two musicals following *Show Boat* are among the proud achievements of the musical stage in the 1930's. In each the theater continues upon its adventurous explorations of the unconventional and the untried, while stripping itself further of much of the encumbering paraphernalia which had been burdening it for so many years.

The Cat and the Fiddle, in 1931, dispensed with chorus girls, production numbers, and formal comedy routines. Set in Brussels, it unfolded a tender love story between a serious Rumanian composer (enacted by Georges Metaxa) and an American girl wild about jazz (played by Bettina Hall). The idea for the play had originated with Otto Harbach, who wrote both text and lyrics. He had hoped to get Sigmund Romberg to write the music, but Romberg was either too busy or too disinterested. But when Kern first heard Harbach outline the idea he rubbed his hair with his hands, betraying his inner excitement. Together, Kern and Harbach worked out some of the plot details, making a conscious effort not merely to create fresh characterizations but also to provide a strong motivation for the music. The English writer, John Agate, later pointed up their success in this aim by maintaining that *The Cat and the Fiddle* was "the first real musical play." In portraying a Rumanian composer in the process of writing an opera Kern was able to spread his wings and venture toward new horizons. At one point he introduced a fugue into his musical texture. A delightful canzonetta, "The Night Was Made For Love" served as a kind of catalyzing agent for the whole play. Equally eloquent lyric moments were achieved with "She Didn't Say Yes," "Poor Pierrot," and "One Moment Alone," to prove that Kern's more ambitious approaches to musical writing did not alienate him from the kind of seductive melodies for which he had so long been famous.

Music in the Air—book and lyrics by Oscar Hammerstein II, and a cast that included Walter Slezak, Tullio Carminati,

Al Shean, and Katherine Carrington—was even more striking than *The Cat and the Fiddle*, for its charming informality and for the way in which music was an inextricable part of play and characters. On the surface it appeared that *Music in the Air* was but one more European-type operetta. It had a picturesque, storybook setting: a small Bavarian town, Edendorff. Its characters were colorful and Germanic: a small town schoolmaster, a conductor of a local choral society, his attractive daughter, an operetta star, the writer of successful operetta librettos. Even the usually stilted operetta plot is not completely avoided: young schoolmaster and his Fräulein are in love; he gets enmeshed in the big city with an operetta star, while his girl friend from Edendorff succumbs to the ambition of becoming a stage star and to the sophistication of a successful writer of operettas. She proves a failure, has to go back home to Edendorff and to her first love, who by this time has also returned to his senses.

Such material is surely shopworn stuff. But skillful tailoring made it a strikingly attractive garment—at any rate for 1933, however outmoded it might appear at a later day. Hammerstein's dialogue, lyrics, and characterizations were filled "with sentiment and comedy that are tender and touching without falling back into the clichés of the trade," remarked Brooks Atkinson. And for his part, Kern produced one of his most lovable scores. "Almost every minute of it is full of . . . mesmeric airs," wrote Percy Hammond. With an increasing expansiveness of style Kern could produce beer hall tunes and simple songs resembling German folk music, melodies which lent authenticity to the play's esoteric setting. On the other hand Kern could gracefully shake from his sleeve such delights as "I've Told Ev'ry Little Star," "The Song Is You," "I'm Alone," and "And Love Was Born," all four with an American identity, but all four so basic to the characters and situations for which they were written that there is never a feeling of incongruity between the American song and the play's Germanic background.

"Mr. Kern and Mr. Hammerstein have discovered," said Brooks Atkinson further in his review, "how musical plays, which used to be assembled, can now be written as organic works of art." He also exclaimed: "At last, musical drama has been emancipated."

Music in the Air played eleven months in New York, was presented in Los Angeles and San Francisco by a West Coast company, and was produced in London in the spring of 1933 by C. B. Cochran.

It cannot be said that time has been as kind to the text of *Music in the Air* as it has been to *Show Boat*. When handsomely revived in 1951 with Dennis King, Jane Pickens, and Charles Winninger, its book was found by most of the critics to be "sparse and dated," "hackneyed playwriting," and "incredible corn." What had once proved so engagingly spontaneous and charming had, in less than two decades, become trite to audiences and critics grown up to plays like *Oklahoma!, Carousel,* and *South Pacific*. But about Kern's music there was still no dissenting voice. In 1951, as eighteen years earlier, it had the fresh bloom of youth. "Although ours is a graceless world," reported Brooks Atkinson, "the lovely Kern score is still full of friendship, patience, cheerfulness and pleasure.... The immortal songs ... still flow through it [the play] like enchanted improvisations. They are part of the theater's richest treasures."

It has often been publicized that Kern derived the basic melodic refrain for "I've Told Ev'ry Little Star" from the song of a finch. Most such stories are fables, but this one is grounded in fact. The episode occurred in 1932 when Kern was a guest at Walter Pollak's summer house in Nantucket.

The bird awakened him late one night with its enchanting refrain. Kern went back to sleep. The following morning he tried unsuccessfully to recall the bird's song. For the next few nights he stayed up until the early hours hoping the bird would return. It finally did, and Kern swiftly put down the *motif* on paper. From his friend Dr. Oliver Austin, a dedicated ornithologist who had a research center in Wellfleet, Massachusetts, Kern discovered that the bird was a finch.

While this story is familiar it is not quite so well known that the opening scene of *Music in the Air* had also been inspired by this bird episode in Nantucket.

Several times before this Kern had found stimulation in bird calls. In his notebook one such fragment appears under date of May 20, 1934, with the following remark: "6 A.M. Bird song from willow tree outside east room." That melodic fragment was used by Kern for something called "Bird of the Peewee." An important two-tone phrase in "Leave it to Jane" is actually a cuckoo's call. In *Sally* Kern had originally intended using the call of the whippoorwill in the melody of his song of the same name, but was finally dissuaded from doing so because a similar phrase appears in George M. Cohan's "Over There."

Despite *The Cat and the Fiddle* and *Music in the Air,* Kern did not abandon a more traditional kind of musical theater. In 1929, two years before *The Cat and the Fiddle,* the partnership of Kern and Hammerstein, which had come into being with *Sunny* and had ripened with *Show Boat,* was revived with the same kind of escapist musical theater with which both had long been identified. Their musical was *Sweet Adeline,* an American period piece described by its authors as "a musical romance of the Gay Nineties." Helen

Morgan, now a stage personality of first importance by virtue of her success as Julie in *Show Boat*, was cast as a singer in her father's beer garden; she becomes a musical-comedy star, gets involved with the backer of her show, but falls in love and marries its composer. To her Kern assigned two of his most winning ballads; the plangent "Why Was I Born?" and "Here Am I." But the tuneful score was also a nostalgic backward glance into the Gay Nineties, especially in such numbers as the waltz ballad, "The Sun About to Rise"; "Play Us a Polka" (a song and dance routine with which the play opens); and a song with a simple American folk character, "'Twas Not So Long Ago."

Sweet Adeline, as Richard Lockridge described it, was a "very pretty and lilting show"; or as Percy Hammond said of it, "a semi-serious and smartly old-fashioned musical, one of the politest frolics of the year." It would surely have enjoyed a success far in excess of its run of 234 performances but for the fact that the stock market crash, in the fall of 1929, made a gay, light, sentimental evening in the theater an anomaly in a world sobered by the harsh realities of an economic debacle. The play would not even have survived these two hundred odd performances were it not that it had profited from an unusually large advance sale.

After Kern had written *The Cat and the Fiddle* and *Music in the Air* he reverted again to a more conventional type of musical production with *Roberta* in 1933. The original plan had been for Hammerstein and Harbach to collaborate on the stage adaptation of Alice Duer Miller's popular novel, *Gowns by Roberta*. (When the Kern musical tried out in Philadelphia it was still called *Gowns by Roberta*. But the title was simplified to *Roberta* by the time the show reached New York because many had mistaken the play for a fashion show.) But since Hammerstein was busily occupied in London, Harbach took on the job himself. To meet certain specific stage needs Harbach made basic changes in the novel. He invented two characters to make more reasonable the presence of music and dance within the play: a crooner-band leader and the manager of the dress establishment who had a gift for dancing. While the play was being cast the decision had been reached to place the venerable Fay Templeton in the title role, in what was to be her last stage appearance after almost half a century of stardom in burlesque and musical comedy. Harbach had to delete her role entirely from the first act and make logical the fact that she was seated throughout the second; such concessions had to be made because in 1933 Fay Templeton weighed two hundred and fifty pounds and could no longer move about freely.

Other significant performers in minor as well as major parts helped make the text of *Roberta* appear livelier, more arresting, and more entertaining than it actually was. Tamara stepped into her first starring role as the designer, Stephanie; she had been discovered in a downtown New York restaurant, the *Kretchma*. A fresh new comic named Bob Hope appeared in the part of Huckleberry Haine; in 1958 Bob Hope revived *Roberta* and his role for television. A young and unknown actor, Fred MacMurray, cast as a member of Hutch's jazz band, proved remarkably adept at imitating the styles of various popular crooners including Rudy Vallee. These three—as well as Ray Middleton as the hero, and George Murphy and Lyda Roberti in secondary roles—lifted a cumbersome and stodgy play out of the doldrums. For despite the efforts of the producer to conceal the fact through a change of title, *Roberta* was little more than a glorified fashion show, its setting a Parisian modiste shop. Even the central love interest seemed incidental to the gowns. That interest involved an American football player—come to Paris to visit his aunt, Roberta, owner of the dress shop—and the shop's designer, Stephanie, who in reality is a Russian princess.

There was something else besides the acting to make *Roberta* a box-office success: a song, "Smoke Gets In Your Eyes," one of Kern's greatest. Kern had first written that melody as a signature for a radio series that never materialized. When a simple, melodious number was required for Stephanie in the second act, in which she recalls her childhood, Kern turned his melody over to Harbach for lyrics. In view of the song's immediate success in the sale of sheet music and records (one of the greatest ever enjoyed by Kern), and since it played so decisive a part in making *Roberta* a box-office success it is interesting to remark that the song was almost dropped from the production even before it was used. At rehearsals, Kern had played the song for the producer, director, and the cast—but in its original version, in strict march rhythm. The decision was negative. Kern was about to reject the song completely when he decided to try it out in a more leisurely tempo and in a sentimental style. Everyone around him realized at once that this was *it*; this was a "natural" for Tamara's caressing, brooding voice. And her delivery was the spot that stopped the show regularly.

Kern often pointed to "Smoke Gets In Your Eyes" as one of his favorites, and it is easy to see why. The diatonic skips in the broad upward sweep of the melody and the seductive change of key in the release that follows never seem to lose their capacity to win the ear and heart. The song was still able to win ear and heart even in an era in which Rock 'n Roll sent ballads into virtual discard. Revived in 1958 by The Platters, "Smoke Gets In Your Eyes" still had the potent appeal of selling over one million records, and occupying the number one spot among the nation's leading song hits for several weeks in 1959.

The immense and sustained popularity of "Smoke Gets In Your Eyes" has tended to obscure the fact that the *Roberta* score possessed another gem in the ballad "Yesterdays" (Fay Templeton's poignant valedictory to the stage; almost as if she herself were casting a nostalgic look backward into her own rich career now coming to an end), with its haunting minor-key mood; and still a third unforgettable Kern song in "The Touch of Your Hand."

When *Roberta* was first transferred to the screen in 1935 by RKO—Fred Astaire and Ginger Rogers in leading roles—Kern consented to include two numbers not in the original stage score. One was "I Won't Dance," an infrequent exercise on Kern's part in rhythmic dexterity, planned for Astaire's nimble toes. The other was an aristocratic ballad, "Lovely to Look At." Pandro Berman and Zion Myers, in charge of production, one day came to Kern's suite at the Beverly-Wilshire to complain that although "Lovely to Look At" was a haunting melody they felt it could never become popular because the refrain was only of sixteen-bar length and also due to the subtle and complex structure of the last four bars. But Kern refused to make any changes. As it turned out, this song became such a hit that when *Roberta* was screened a second time—in 1952 by M-G-M with Kathryn Grayson, Red Skelton, and Howard Keel—it was called *Lovely to Look At.*

Six years separated *Roberta* from Kern's next Broadway musical, *Very Warm for May,* book and lyrics by Oscar Hammerstein II. As it turned out, *Very Warm for May* was the last musical Kern wrote for Broadway. One would have hoped that the end of one of the most lustrous careers in the history of the American musical theater had taken place under happier auspices and had been more worthy of a man, who more than any single person had helped to direct the destiny of that theater. *Very Warm for May* suffered from a trite and rambling yarn about a badly managed New England stock company, and the love complications of two children of its performers for two people of high society. (It should, however, be pointed out that when the play first tried out in Wilmington, Delware, and Washington, D.C., it had a far different, far more original, and far more appealing text than the one with which it opened in New York. But the producer, Max Gordon, and the stage director, Vincente Minnelli, both became convinced that the play as originally written had no commercial appeal and insisted upon drastic revisions during which the play was emasculated—completely changed and not to its advantage.) "The book," said Brooks Atkinson, "is a singularly haphazard invention that throws the whole show out of focus and makes an appreciation of Mr. Kern's music almost a challenge." Other critics also did not mince words. Richard Watts, Jr. found the book "excessively tedious and humorless," and Richard Lockridge considered the plot "thoroughly exasperating." (A lonely vote in favor of the play was cast by John Anderson.) In the face of such onslaught *Very Warm for May* collapsed after only fifty-nine performances. On the second night there were only twenty people in the theater. A day after that, when Kern went down to the theater to console the cast, he found Max Gordon in the lobby frantically computing how much he was losing on the production.

But *Very Warm for May* was not completely a deficit as far as Kern was concerned. His inventive score—highlighted by some strikingly original dance episodes, including a classic gavotte—boasted one of the greatest songs to emerge from the American musical stage, "All the Things You Are." Original in its intervallic structure and subtle and magical in its enharmonic changes, "All the Things You Are" was written by Kern more for his own artistic satisfaction than to woo a public, since he himself was convinced when he wrote it that it could never become popular. Yet after its appearance "All the Things You Are" became one of Kern's hardiest successes in the sale of sheet music and records.

Very Warm for May, in 1939, marked the end of what might reasonably be described as the Kern epoch in the American musical theater. That epoch spanned thirty-five years. Nobody before Kern had enjoyed such an extended activity as a composer for the American musical stage; nobody before him had been personally involved in and responsible for such dramatic changes in the traditions of the American musical comedy; and nobody before him—not even the redoubtable Victor Herbert—had produced so much music and had achieved with it such striking successes.

In those thirty-five years Kern had written either the complete or the major part of the scores of thirty-eight Broadway musicals; he had also interpolated songs in about fifty other productions. From the perspective of time, musicals like *The Girl from Utah, Very Good, Eddie, Oh Boy!, Sally, Sunny, Show Boat, The Cat and the Fiddle, Roberta,* and *Music in the Air* shine against the background of the American theater like ornaments on a Christmas tree. Within these productions were found hundreds of songs. "They Didn't Believe Me," "Till the Clouds Roll By," "Who?", "Bill," "Can't Help Lovin' That Man," "Ol' Man River," "Why Was I Born?", "The Night Was Made for Love," "I've Told Ev'ry Little Star," "The Song Is You," "Smoke Gets In Your Eyes," "Yesterdays," and "All the Things You Are"—these are only

End of an Epoch 113

an armful of the many songs by which Kern's majestic place in American music was made secure.

A supplementary word on the Kern epoch in the American theater should be added at this point. The music to three other significant Broadway productions might have been written by Kern but for varying circumstances. Since each of these three musicals in its own way has had historic importance in the American theater, the fact that they might have been Kern's provides a fascinating footnote to the history of the Broadway theater and to a Kern biography. The Kern admirer can hardly resist succumbing to the fascinating, if fruitless, speculation of what each of these plays might have been like if Kern, instead of other composers, had been involved with them.

The first was George Gershwin's monumental folk opera, *Porgy and Bess.* Gershwin and DuBose Heyward had for several years been discussing the plan to transform the latter's novel and play, *Porgy,* into an opera, before finally settling down to work. Suddenly, the Theater Guild—producers of the play—began formulating plans of its own. It was considering converting *Porgy* into a musical comedy starring Al Jolson. With this in mind it wanted Kern to write the score and Oscar Hammerstein II the book and lyrics. Since Gershwin recognized the financial potential of such a venture for DuBose Heyward (who, at the time, was in a difficult financial position) he graciously offered to step aside from their projected opera collaboration to permit the musical-comedy version to achieve fruition. But despite his desperate need for money, DuBose Heyward was more interested in the serious artistic venture that the Gershwin opera promised to be than in a commercial bonanza that a Kern-Hammerstein musical comedy with Al Jolson certainly would have become. The deal for the musical comedy, consequently, fell through.

A decade later Oscar Hammerstein II approached Kern with a new project close to his heart: the adaptation of still another Theater Guild play, Lynn Riggs' *Green Grow the Lilacs*, into a musical. Hammerstein read Kern the play at Kern's swimming pool in Beverly Hills, hoping to fire him with his own excitement. But Kern remained cold. He felt the musical problems posed by that play were too tricky for successful resolution. *Green Grow the Lilacs* was, nonetheless, carried triumphantly into the musical theater as *Oklahoma!*, book and lyrics by Hammerstein but with music by Richard Rodgers.

The third historic production on which Kern might have been engaged was *Annie Get Your Gun*. When the new producing firm of Rodgers and Hammerstein first planned a musical based on the colorful personality of Annie Oakley they asked Kern to do the music. Kern, absent from Broadway for over half-a-dozen years, eagerly consented. But before he could put a single note on paper he was stricken by his last fatal illness. The musical assignment was inherited by Irving Berlin who achieved with it the greatest stage score of his resplendent career and his most resounding box-office triumph (1,147 performances in New York).

14

Hollywood

Kern's career on Broadway ended in 1939. Meanwhile a new one had begun in Hollywood in 1931. From 1939 on he channeled his musical energies into the motion-picture industry.

When, in the late 1920's, the screen first burst into sound it placed particular significance upon musical productions. Studios competed savagely with one another to acquire suitable properties for motion-picture adaptation. Many of the successful—and even some of the less successful—productions of the Broadway stage were scooped up by Hollywood's avaricious arms. In this process several of Kern's most famous Broadway musicals were transferred to the screen: *Show Boat* and *Sally* in 1929, the latter with Marilyn Miller in her original stage role; *Sunny*, once again with Marilyn Miller, in 1930; *The Cat and the Fiddle* in 1933; *Music in the Air* in 1934; *Roberta* with Fred Astaire and Ginger Rogers; *Sweet Adeline* in 1935; *Show Boat* again in 1936; *Sunny* again in 1941; *Show Boat* again in 1951; and

Roberta again in 1952, now renamed *Lovely to Look At*.

But Hollywood was also busily engaged in producing original screen musicals. Once again it reached across the country to lift from Broadway its most important composers, lyricists, and librettists. Being leaders in their respective fields in American popular music, Kern and Otto Harbach were among the first to be called. In 1931 they were contracted by the RKO studios to write original songs for *Men in the Sky*. This visit to Hollywood was fraught with disappointment and frustration for both men. They completed a score on which they had labored painstakingly to find a logical story motivation for each of the songs. Yet when *Men in the Sky* was finally released, most of the songs were discarded and others were used only as background music.

The reason this happened was that in 1932 many Hollywood producers had come to the conclusion that motion-picture audiences had grown weary of screen musicals. This was also the reason Kern did not return to Hollywood for another assignment for two years or more. But he was back in Hollywood in 1934, settling in an eighth-floor suite at the Beverly-Wilshire Hotel, his home for the next three years. His first major project was on the RKO lot, where he was assigned a musical starring Lily Pons, *I Dream Too Much*. It was on this occasion that he first met André Kostelanetz (Lily Pons' husband), a conductor who has often distinguished himself in performances of Kern's music. This association soon blossomed into warm friendship. At that first meeting Kostelanetz was particularly impressed by a vein of humility which Kern occasionally revealed to fellow musicians whom he admired particularly, by expressing to Kostelanetz his unworthiness to write music for an opera star like Lily Pons.

Between 1934 and 1938 Kern wrote two more scores for

RKO: *Swing Time* with Fred Astaire and Ginger Rogers and *Joy of Living* with Irene Dunne. He also worked for Columbia in an operetta starring Grace Moore, *When You're In Love;* and for Paramount in a second Irene Dunne musical, *High, Wide and Handsome.*

With *I Dream Too Much*, Kern began a collaboration with the lyricist, Dorothy Fields, which proved for him a consistently happy experience. He admired Dorothy Fields' skill with the written word, and he found her a sensitive and sympathetic coworker. Dorothy Fields, of course, belonged to the celebrated theatrical family headed by her father, Lew Fields, former member of Weber and Fields, and after that a successful Broadway actor and producer. Dorothy's brothers, Herbert and Joseph, enjoyed distinguished careers in the Broadway theater as playwrights and librettists. Dorothy, youngest of the Fields children, made her bow as a lyricist when she formed a successful song-writing partnership with Jimmy McHugh in *Blackbirds of 1928.* Her Broadway successes with McHugh brought her to Hollywood, and in 1934 her first association with Kern as lyricist. Among the successful numbers they wrote for *I Dream Too Much* were the title song, "Jockey on the Carousel," and "I'm the Echo, You're the Song."

Dorothy Fields continued working fruitfully with Kern in *Swing Time, Joy of Living,* and *When You're in Love,* and their partnership ended in 1940 with three songs for *One Night in the Tropics.*

Kern was not at first happy working for motion pictures. He had too keen a sense of good theater and too much respect for freshness of material and original techniques not to know what was vitally wrong with most of the pictures in which he was involved. He felt smothered by the fact he was never consulted for advice or criticism or a script. At the same time he was continually faced by directors and producers trying to tell him how to write his music.

But there were occasions when he was delighted with a picture and enjoyed immensely writing music for it and its stars. One such occasion was in 1935 with *Swing Time*. Fred Astaire and Ginger Rogers were at the height of their popularity. The sprightly script by Howard Lindsay and Allan Scott was studded with smart lines and delightful situations arising from a gambling hoofer's interest in and pursuit of a prim dance instructress. Such a story was beautifully sculptured for the charm of Astaire and Rogers and their incomparable way with a song and a dance. Fred Astaire did an exciting dance in blackface against a background of provocative shadows, and with Ginger Rogers participated in a broad burlesque on dance lessons. Victor Moore—as Astaire's man Friday—also contributed a hilarious dance sequence with Helen Broderick. The sum total was, as Howard Barnes reported, "an enchanting and amusing kaleidoscope of nimble feet, lilting melodies, and humorous invention."

There was always a direct ratio between the quality of music Kern produced for any given motion picture and his enthusiasm for that assignment. Kern's score for *Swing Time* to Dorothy Fields' sprightly lyrics proved to be the most infectious he created in Hollywood. It included "Bojangles of Harlem," "Pick Yourself Up," "A Fine Romance," and the song with which he won the Academy Award for the first time, "The Way You Look Tonight."

Curiously, "The Way You Look Tonight," which became famous as a love ballad, was used in the picture as a comedy number to ridicule Ginger Rogers, as Penny, on her unsightly appearance while she was shampooing her hair.

15

Life at Fifty

Mark Holstein and William Kron made the cross-country trip to help Kern celebrate his fiftieth birthday on Sunday, January 27, 1935. That morning Kern informed Eva he had to go out with Holstein and Kron on a real-estate deal. Actually this was a deception; he was planning to surprise Eva. Elsie Pollak, to whom Eva was especially devoted, was arriving that day from New York and Kern wanted to pick her up at the Pasadena railroad station and bring her back to the hotel without warning Eva about it.

Eva was considerably put out to hear Kern say he was going out on business. She, too, had a surprise to spring. Alexander Woollcott, then so popular over the radio as the Town Crier, had made her promise that Kern would listen that day—at 4 p.m. California time—to his broadcast from New York, since he was planning a birthday tribute. But Woollcott also insisted that Eva keep this matter a dark secret so that the broadcast might fall on Kern's unsuspecting ears. Kern's decision to go out on "real-estate business" threatened to upset these carefully prepared arrangements. Eva begged her husband to postpone his operations for some other time and to stay home on his birthday. When she failed, she made him promise that at the very least he would be back at the hotel no later than 3 p.m.

A little after three Eva turned on the radio to await the four o'clock Woollcott broadcast. But still there was no sight or sound of Jerry. She and Betty watched the clock with increasing anguish. Suddenly, at a quarter to four, Kern burst into the suite with Elsie, Holstein, and Kron. Impatiently, Kern went over to the radio and turned it off, growling that the noise was blasting him clear out into Wilshire Boulevard. As Eva went into the kitchen to prepare some tea for her guests she sidled over to the radio and turned it on again. Kern strode angrily across the room to turn it off when, suddenly, his movements were arrested by the sound of his own music. When the music died down he heard Woollcott's voice announcing:

> the first as far as I know in the history of the microphone— a surprise party to celebrate the birthday of one who by this time may be beginning to suspect that he is the occasion of all this mystery. He is in a hotel on the other side of the continent from us and may even now be gazing at his family in his first wild surmise, unless perhaps he had already been put on his guard by the melodies with which this broadcast was ushered on to the air. Fifty years ago today something happened in New York which, however little anyone suspected it at the time, was destined to add considerably to the enjoyment of existence on earth. Fifty years ago—1885— a node in the vibrations of the nineteenth century—a lull in the hubbub of history.... Jerome Kern came into the world with his head full of tunes and the world has been a pleasanter place on that account.

Then, during the next twenty minutes or so, an orchestra played a Kern medley: Julia Sanderson sang "They Didn't Believe Me" the way she had done in 1914 in *The Girl from Utah;* and Walter Slezak repeated his rendition of "I've Told Ev'ry Little Star" from *Music in the Air;* Noel Coward (whom Kern had befriended, and for whose career Kern had provided a helping hand when Coward was still young, struggling, and unknown) presented "Till the Clouds Roll By" as a tribute to "my favorite composer"; Alice Duer Miller read an ode written expressly for the occasion by the beloved columnist and wit, F.P.A.; Kathleen Norris and Ethel Barrymore delivered birthday messages.

Then as the program drew to a close Woollcott quietly told Kern:

> even now, let me see, yes in Beverly Hills, it's twenty-six minutes past four, even now a messenger is getting out of the elevator on your floor in the Beverly-Wilshire with flowers in his arms. . . . He's starting down the corridor towards your rooms looking like a flower girl at a wedding. In another ten seconds you should hear him knock on the door. Take my advice, Mr. Kern, and don't send anyone to answer that knock. You go and open the door yourself. For we have chosen as our messenger one who has himself done a little something in the field of words and music, but this time he will say it with flowers. Have you heard his knock? Then go yourself and let him in, for our messenger's name is—Irving Berlin.

As the radio chanted the soft accompaniment of strains from "Ol' Man River" Kern went to the door and burst into tears. After he had somewhat recovered his composure and opened several bottles of champagne for the occasion Kern remarked simply: "Isn't it wonderful to be eulogized while you're still alive to hear and enjoy it?"

In the ensuing years Kern continually referred to this Sunday afternoon birthday party as one of the high moments of his life; and he remained grateful to Woollcott for having made it possible.

About a year before this fiftieth birthday celebration Kern had begun to suffer from physical weakness, general lassitude, loss of weight, and increasing irritability. Most of his adult life Kern had been addicted to consulting doctors and had been victimized by a subconscious fear that some day he might succumb to anemia as his father had done (and from which he himself had been suffering mildly on and off for many years), or like his mother to cancer. But after further deterioration of his health in 1934, it was discovered by Dr. Foster Kennedy that he was now actually a victim of pernicious anemia. With Dr. Kennedy's help Kern was slowly nursed back to health, and by the time he reached his fiftieth birthday was fully recovered. From then on Dr. Kennedy was one of Kern's close friends and the one to whom he reached whenever he became sick.

By the time he was over this malady he had come to love California for its climate, scenic beauty, and placid way of life. He had even grown mellow and tolerant of motion-picture methods, content with his place in Hollywood's scheme of things. Now determined to spend the rest of his life in California, he had built for himself and his family, in 1937, a luxurious, white brick house at 917 Whittier Drive in Beverly Hills.

One week after the Kerns moved to their new home, in May, 1937—and while it was still in the disordered state of being furnished—Kern once again fell seriously ill. At a pleasant Saturday evening dinner with the Irving Berlins he had shown no signs that anything was wrong. But the following morning, immediately after breakfast, he complained of exhaustion and feeling faint. Dr. Samuel Hirshfeld immediately diagnosed Kern's sickness as a coronary thrombosis. Twenty-one days later Kern also suffered a paralytic stroke.

For months he was completely incapacitated, a partially paralyzed invalid, attended night and day by a round of nurses; from the beginning Dr. Hirshfeld was in constant communication with Dr. Foster Kennedy in New York to determine the required treatment. The physicians permitted only Eva, Dorothy Fields, and Oscar Hammerstein (then living in Beverly Hills) to see him, and then only briefly; Betty was completely denied access to her father for fear her presence might prove too much of an emotional upheaval. For a person as gregarious as Kern such solitary confinement proved almost as harrowing as his physical disintegration. Perhaps because of that solitude he succumbed to deep depressions; also to a crushing guilt complex that he had never been to his parents as good a son as they deserved.

But slowly, and with time, his condition began to mend, and his spirits lifted. He now sought diversion in bird lore, collecting stamps, and making bets on the horses with bookmakers over the telephone. The first letter he wrote during that illness was early in the summer to George Gershwin, having heard that Gershwin was seriously ill. "They have been keeping me in cellophane and absorbent cotton," Kern wrote Gershwin, "and shielding me from all distressing news. So it was only yesterday that I heard of your trouble. I hasten to send you my best wishes for the speediest and completest recovery." Kern was carefully shielded from the news of Gershwin's death on July 11, 1937, but it was apparent to Eva that somehow he had learned about it.

About nine months after he had first fallen ill Kern tried

playing the piano again. "That was probably the worst experience of my life," says Eva, recalling the abrupt, halting, and at times discordant sounds that stumbled from Kern's studio and drifted upward to Eva's bedroom. But this was nevertheless an encouraging sign, an important step forward in his recovery. Before long he was playing the piano more often and more accurately. And finally he was back again writing songs.

16

New Horizons

In the next half-dozen years Kern demonstrated again and again that his serious and prolonged illness had not tarnished the quality of his inspiration. In his best songs for motion pictures he could still tap that rich and sensitive creative vein uniquely his: "Dearly Beloved" (lyrics by Johnny Mercer) from Rita Hayworth's film, *You Were Never Lovelier;* "Long Ago and Far Away" (words by Ira Gershwin, who here scored his biggest commercial hit) for another Rita Hayworth picture, *Cover Girl;* "And Russia Is Her Name" (E. Y. Harburg) from *Song of Russia,* but first introduced by Jan Peerce and the André Kostelanetz Orchestra over the CBS network in June, 1942, to commemorate the first anniversary of the Nazi invasion of the Soviet Union; "More and More" (E. Y. Harburg) from *Can't Help Singing* with Deanna Durbin; and, perhaps most significant of all, "The Last Time I Saw Paris" (Hammerstein).

"The Last Time I Saw Paris" was unique among Kern's

songs in that the lyric was written before the music. Oscar Hammerstein II had known Paris from his boyhood days when he had accompanied his father on a talent-hunting trip and stayed at the Grand Hotel; he grew intimate with the city in early manhood when for five months he occupied an apartment near the Etoile. Therefore when, in June 1940, during World War II, France capitulated to the Nazis—and Hitler, as a conqueror, surveyed Paris from the terrace of the Hôtel des Invalides—Hammerstein was so stirred he found it impossible to concentrate on *Sunny River,* a musical comedy he was then writing with Sigmund Romberg. Not until he had been able to put down on paper a poignant lyric about the city of his dreams and memories was he able to find emotional release from his heartache.

Soon after finishing the lyric of "The Last Time I Saw Paris" Hammerstein left for Beverly Hills to discuss *Sunny River* with Romberg. At that time Hammerstein confided to Romberg that he planned to ask Kern to write the music for his lyric about Paris. Kern wrote his music only one day after Hammerstein had shown him the lyric, and virtually in a single sitting.

The first performance of "The Last Time I Saw Paris" was given by Kate Smith on her radio program. Since she had been given a six-week exclusive on the song nobody else could present it over the radio in that time. Soon after the termination of this six-week period ASCAP, in a bitter contractual dispute with the radio networks, placed a ban on performances over radio of music by its members. This ban closed the air channels to "The Last Time I Saw Paris." But the song nonetheless became exceptionally popular. Hildegarde issued a remarkable recording—personally supervised by Kern himself—which enjoyed a fabulous sale. Hildegarde also presented the song with extraordinary effect in supper and night clubs, as did Noel Coward and Sophie Tucker, among others.

"The Last Time I Saw Paris" was unusual among Kern's songs for a reason other than that the lyric preceded the melody. It was also the only Kern song not written for a specific stage or screen production. Nevertheless, it was interpolated into a motion picture, *Lady Be Good*, in 1941, an old George and Ira Gershwin Broadway musical adapted for the screen, with Ann Sothern, Eleanor Powell, and Robert Young. Though it was the only Kern song in a score that included three Gershwin numbers and two others by Roger Edens, "The Last Time I Saw Paris" (presented by Ann Sothern) won the Academy Award that year.

Whatever exhilaration Kern might have felt in winning an Academy Award a second time was considerably diluted by his conviction that Harold Arlen should have won it that year with his remarkable song from *Star-Spangled Rhythm*, "That Old Black Magic"; and that "The Last Time I Saw Paris" was not deserving of an Academy Award since it had not been written expressly for motion pictures. It was characteristic of Kern that feeling as he did, he should immediately have become the prime mover in changing the Academy Award rules so that only songs written expressly for motion pictures be henceforth eligible.

At the same time he was producing such notable songs Kern was also enlarging the scope and dimensions of his writing by completing projects for string quartet and symphony orchestra. In 1940-1941 he transcribed for string quartet (with the assistance of Charles Miller) several of his songs: "All the Things You Are," "The Way You Look Tonight," "Smoke Gets In Your Eyes," "Yesterdays," "Once in a Blue Moon," "The Song Is You," and "Bill." These transcriptions were made at the behest of Jack Kapp, head of Decca Records, and were recorded for Decca by the Gordon String Quartet.

In 1941 Kern wrote *Scenario*, the symphonic adaptation and enlargement of melodies from *Show Boat*, already mentioned. Before he turned the completed score over to Artur Rodzinski, the conductor who had commissioned it and who was introducing it in Cleveland, Kern tried out his music with the David Meremblum Children's Orchestra in Hollywood. Kern's experience with that orchestra proved so rewarding that he instituted for that organization an annual scholarship for gifted musical children.

One of the proudest moments in Kern's life came when Rodzinski gave the New York première of *Scenario* with the New York Philharmonic on November 19, 1941. Kern, who had come to New York for the performance, was called upon to step from his seat, mount the stage of Carnegie Hall, and respond to a rousing ovation from a serious concert audience.

Soon after Pearl Harbor, André Kostelanetz called upon Kern to write another symphonic work, this time with original melodic materials, and inspired by some great American. This was one of several orchestral works on American subjects commissioned by Kostelanetz from important American composers "to mirror," as he put it, "the magnificent spirit of our country. The greatness of a nation is expressed through its people, and those people who have achieved greatness are the logical subjects for a series of musical portraits." (One of these, *Lincoln Portrait*, was written for Kostelanetz by Aaron Copland; another, the *Mayor La Guardia Waltzes*, by Virgil Thomson.) The recent success of *Scenario* in performances by several major American orchestras made Kern more receptive to such an ambitious project than he might otherwise have been. For his American subject Kern chose one of his literary idols, Mark Twain.

Composition soon absorbed Kern completely. As he wrote to Kostelanetz: "All else is laid aside in my tremendous enthusiasm for our project which for the past forty-eight hours or so has made me wellnigh breathless." As he kept on working, he showered Kostelanetz with letters explaining what he was doing and why. "Kern took nothing for granted," says Kostelanetz, "left nothing to chance. Every line of the score was planned and motivated. And he kept on working on the most minute details of his work not only to the very moment he dispatched the manuscript to me, but even afterwards."

Immediately after the première performance, which took place in Cincinnati on May 14, 1942, Kostelanetz conducting the Cincinnati Symphony, Kern dispatched the following wire to the conductor: "In my delight, completely forgot to suggest you raise bass of bar 341 to D-sharp, which then slides into E-natural of the bar of 345 unnoticeably." This was followed by a detailed letter pointing out to Kostelanetz what had sounded well in the performance and what had missed aim. But Kern was not the man to regard anything he wrote as so much life's blood, even a work so serious in purpose and so ambitious in design as *Mark Twain: A Portrait for Orchestra*. As Kostelanetz says:

> Though he was as fastidious about his work as a master craftsman, there was no suggestion of temperament about him, no pigheaded stubbornness when others had an improvement to suggest.... Once as a matter of fact, he took me to task for playing his music with too strict an adherence to his own intentions. "When you next program it, how about a little more Kostelanetz, and a little less Kern? Mind you, I'm not being coy. Between us there is no room for nonsense

of that sort. You were a mite too respectful. More of the Kostelanetz dash and fire sounds mighty agreeable to these old ears."

The work is in four movements or episodes. The first "Hannibal Days" describes a "white town . . . drowsing in the sunshine of a summer morning, ninety years ago." Kern's program goes on to explain: "Ste-e-am-boat Comin'! The town awakens. . . . Minutes later the steamer is under way again, the town dozes off." In the second part, "Gorgeous Pilot House," Mark leaves his home to fulfill a boyhood ambition of becoming a Pilot's assistant. "Mark's piping call as a leadman is heard: 'M-a-r-k T-w-a-i-n!' It develops in grandiose fashion covering his nine years of full-fledged piloting. It is all shattered by the coming of the war in 1861." This is followed by "Wandering Westward," in which Twain becomes a prospector in Nevada, meets failure, and turns to journalism and his first use of the pseudonym, Mark Twain. In the finale, "Mark in Eruption," we follow Mark Twain's triumphant career as a writer, his visit to England to receive an honorary degree from Oxford, his meetings with European royalty. "Still the music recalls the river theme and the pilot house as a reminder that this honored great American man of letters never lost his nostalgia for the Mississippi and the river boats."

Scenario and *Mark Twain* are the only two concert works for orchestra by Kern. Neither is of special distinction, though *Scenario* has sufficient melodic vitality to warrant occasional revival by symphony orchestras. Kern knew his strength and shortcomings when he preferred concentrating on the stage and screen within designs often no more ambitious than the thirty-two bar chorus. His strength was his formidable melodic invention, his seemingly inexhaustible supply of winning lyric ideas; and this remains the strongest asset of his two symphonic works. But he did not have the skill to create an organic unity of his material, nor did he possess the gift of thematic development. Both *Scenario* and *Mark Twain* are kaleidoscopic, with passing flashes of interesting or arresting colors and schemes. They are pleasant experiences to the ear in much the same way that kaleidoscopes are to the eye—but in both cases the experiences are ephemeral. Even if a passing thought or two has fascination the fact remains that neither *Scenario* nor *Mark Twain* is an integrated artistic concept; and for this reason their survival in the symphonic repertory is extremely doubtful.

Two other symphonic works, while actually not by Kern himself, were based on Kern's music and deserve attention. Both are by Robert Russell Bennett, who was also responsible for the brilliant orchestrations of several of Kern's stage scores including *Music in the Air*, *Very Warm for May*, and the 1948 revival of *Show Boat*. In 1934 Bennett wrote the *Variations on a Theme by Jerome Kern* for orchestra, which soon after its completion was introduced by Bernard Herrmann and his chamber orchestra in Town Hall, New York. The theme used here was "Once in a Blue Moon" from *Stepping Stones*. In 1946 Bennett created a tone poem entitled *Symphonic Study* (first performed that year over the NBC network, Frank Black conducting). This was a symphonic synthesis of several of Kern's best-loved melodies, presented chronologically. The work opened with "They Didn't Believe Me" and ended with "All the Things You Are." In between were heard several other Kern songs including, "Babes in the Wood," "The Siren's Song," "Left All Alone Again Blues," "Who?", "Ol' Man River," and "Smoke Gets In Your Eyes."

17

Grand Seigneur of Beverly Hills

Since Kern had been responsible for most of the architectural features of his house and since he had also had a commanding hand in its furnishings it is not surprising to find it so much a reflection of his own personality. The white-washed brick house on Whittier Drive had a baronial air—large, rambling, comfortable. But there was nothing about it to seize the eye; nothing there that was ostentatious or sumptuous or exotic in the style of so many Beverly Hills houses nearby. Kern had brought from his Bronxville house most of the furnishings of which he was especially fond: the handsome, stately period pieces; the two grand pianos; the seventeenth-century paintings; the abundant photographs and books and objets d' art; the almost pell-mell scattering of decorative goblets, silver, china assembled almost like an improvisation. The furnishings at Whittier Drive thus never had the symmetry and formality of design to betray the skillful hand of the interior decorator. It was almost

Grand Seigneur of Beverly Hills

haphazard in its decorative scheme, generally overcrowded with the things Kern liked having around him whether or not they happened to conform to some unified pattern of decoration. And the place radiated the same geniality, warmth, cultured grace, and winning informality that the hosts did. It was a place lending itself not to huge formal dinners and extravagant parties which, truth to tell, the Kerns avoided like the plague, but to informal gatherings of good friends such as Harry Cohn, the Irving Berlins, Harold Arlen, Arthur Schwartz, Cole Porter, Johnny Green, the Ira Gershwins, David Tannenbaum (Kern's Hollywood lawyer), and others who relaxed there with amusing and stimulating talk.

The favorite rendezvous of Kern's closest friends—and Kern's own favorite in his house—was the ample studio of his working hours, but which soon became the place for all his indoor relaxation as well. Like so many other rooms in the house, this one gave a crowded impression. The walls were lined with autographed photographs of many of Kern's friends, associates, and admirers, including Leopold Stokowski, Dimitri Mitropoulos, Noel Coward, and Lord and Lady Mountbatten. The bookshelves overflowed, several of them holding rare editions or presentation copies of Dickens, Darwin, Sir James Barrie, and others, which Kern had begun to acquire as soon as he had disposed of his entire million-dollar book collection in 1929. In this room there was a small, well-stocked bar where Kern liked to serve Irish Whiskey or mix drinks for his friends; he himsef enjoyed Scotch or champagne.

In this room Kern kept his recording machine, radio and phonograph, big comfortable chairs. Here, too, was his grand piano with an attached desk. On the extreme sides of the keyboard stood miniature busts of Wagner and Liszt. "I can always tell when I've written a good tune," Kern once said, "for then Wagner breaks out into a broad grin." A couch enabled Kern to sprawl out leisurely while reading a book or listening to the phonograph or radio, dictating to his secretary, or working with one of his collaborators. At convenient nearby tables always stood his collection of pipes and an ample supply of cigarettes. Kern was an addicted smoker, but from time to time he would give up the habit for brief periods to test his will power. Candy and sweets were also a weakness, especially when he was working.

The curious part about this well-equipped studio—the slightest fixture and appointment of which had been meticulously planned by Kern—is that he had completely forgotten to make allowance for shelves tall enough to hold his music scores, manuscripts, and phonograph records. Consequently, the room was usually in a happy state of disorder, with music, manuscripts, and records piled all over the piano, on the floor, or on any convenient protruding ledge. In time, these piles overflowed across the hall into the living room and down into the basement. The pell-mell confusion in the study was always a source of irritation to Eva. One day while she was out, Kern decided to surprise her by putting the room in order. When she returned, he conducted her proudly to his study and amazed her with its trim neatness. But her joy was short-lived. A few minutes later she discovered that Kern had transferred the overflow of books, magazines, records, newspapers, and sheet music from his study to the living room floor.

In Beverly Hills, as formerly in New York, one of his main diversions (outside of sitting around till all hours of the night conversing with friends) was playing poker. He had a special card room, built somewhat apart from the other rooms so that the rowdy spirits of the players need not disturb the family. It always amused his friends how considerate he was in protecting his family from such noises, in view of the fact that when the game was over early in the morning he would often go right into his studio and spend the next few hours banging lustily on the piano. He was also a regular participant in Saturday evening poker games with a few friends, including Ira Gershwin, Marc Connelly, Arthur Kober, Howard Benedict, George Haight, and Eugene Solow. These games took place, at different periods, at the Beverly-Wilshire where a room was rented weekly for this purpose, at Ted Snyder's restaurant on Sunset Boulevard, or at an apartment which for a long time they maintained just for cards. "I think," Kern once wrote wearily to Ira Gershwin, "five or six hours in a smoke-filled room, struggling for existence against the aggressors is perhaps a little arduous for this dilapidated chassis and weary, ancient bones." But he came regularly nevertheless—and was usually most vocal in demanding an additional last round for "Russel Crouse's grandmother," a phrase and an excuse conveniently contrived by the players to allow a final round for the losers, among whom Kern was invariably the most prominent.

He was still an addict of parlor games, of making bets on horses either through bookmakers or at the Santa Anita Track, or perpetrating jokes. He still liked wearing outlandish costumes: a favorite one in Beverly Hills was a blue coat with brass buttons, a Heidelberg student's cap, and a Paisley cravat. But some habits had changed. His one time interest in golf had been replaced by sessions at a pitch-and-putt course in the Holmby Hills section between Beverly Hills and Westwood with Harold Arlen, Gus Kahn, and Harry Warren among others. He would go "pitching" around that miniature course with the enthusiasm of a boy with an ingenious toy—only as he used to put it "with me the vowel in pitching is wrong; it's more potching than pitching."

He had also long since given up driving his car. In fact, he almost never used his own car when he had to go anywhere, preferring to hire a chauffeur-driven vehicle. Once he hired such a car to take him out to the Rose Bowl game. But as soon as he got there and saw the crowds pouring into the Bowl, he had the car take him back home where he could hear the game peacefully over the radio.

One other significant change took place in Kern's personal life in Beverly Hills. Eva now began to move freely in his professional circles, something she had never done in Bronxville; and for the first time he had begun to consult her about his business deals and to lean on her advice and judgment.

As a salute to Kern's magisterial place in American music (a place recognized by the National Institute of Arts and Letters when it elected him to membership in 1944), Hollywood soon began planning his screen biography. This project was born with Arthur Freed at M-G-M. Kern himself was from the first skeptical about the practicability of such a venture. "How can they dramatize my life when nothing happened to me?" he would ask. "I'm much too normal. I lead much too dull and conventional a life. And I've had only one wife." Besides he was convinced that a picture about Jerome Kern had very little commercial appeal because, he insisted, few people knew who Kern was. "Yes, they know my songs," he told Freed, "but not the name of the man who wrote them." In fact Kern tried to convince Freed to consider a biography in which the main character bore a fictitious name. "A good idea," was Ira Gershwin's wry comment to Freed. "Call him J. Fred Coots."

Despite Kern's own doubts, plans for the picture went ahead. Freed early decided to call on Guy Bolton to write the story. In discussing the casting, Kern himself was partial toward having Burgess Meredith portray him, but this suggestion had to be discarded when Kern realized Meredith would not fit the part of the younger Kern. The final choice of Robert Walker met with the immediate approval of both Kern and his wife. The part of Eva was assumed by Dorothy Patrick; Paul Langton played Oscar Hammerstein II, and Paul Maxey, Victor Herbert.

Till the Clouds Roll By, as the screen biography was finally called, was not released until over a year after Kern's death, and Kern did not live to see most of the plans for the picture jell, or to approve those plans, although he had read Guy Bolton's script. That script, like most such cinematic biographies, was merely a convenience for the presentation of Kern's songs. Biographical truth was sidestepped as the story itself followed a recognizable stereotype of sentimentality and romance. "If you had told the truth," Kern told Bolton with sympathetic understanding, "it would have been the dullest picture in the world."

The picture opened with songs and episodes from *Show Boat*, then cut back to the turn of the century when Kern—young, unknown, ambitious—was inspired to great achievements by a lifelong friend. What follows after that is, as Bosley Crowther said in the New York *Times*, "a thoroughly phoney yarn about the struggles of a chirping young composer," treated in such a "hackneyed and sentimental way as to grate on the sensibilities of even the most affectionately disposed."

But *Till the Clouds Roll By* was nevertheless a memorable screen achievement, since it was a mighty caravan of Kern riches. Twenty-two of his greatest songs were presented, from the early "How'd You Like to Spoon With Me?" through the comparatively late "Long Ago and Far Away"—and they were presented by star performers who included Lena Horne, Frank Sinatra, Dinah Shore, Cyd Charisse, Tony Martin, Kathryn Grayson, June Allyson, and Judy Garland.

"The song is you," reads a key phrase in one of Kern's best-known songs. The songs *were* Kern. In *Till the Clouds Roll By* the Kern songs told his story more authentically and more poignantly than any synthetic tale of struggle and romance.

18

"When He Goes Away, Dat's a Rainy Day"

Kern had every reason to be satisfied with himself and optimistic about his future, when late in 1945 he planned an important trip to New York. He had recently completed a new, excellent score (which included songs like "In Love In Vain," "All Through the Day," and "Two Hearts are Better than One") for a 20th Century-Fox motion-picture, *Centennial Summer*. He had been the object of a monumental Jerome Kern Jubilee, celebrated throughout the United States between December 11 and 17, 1944, with performances of his songs in theaters and night clubs and over the radio. And as perhaps the most fitting summation of past achievements, his screen biography was being produced at M-G-M by Arthur Freed.

All this was eloquent testimony of how much he had accomplished by his sixtieth birthday. But satisfaction with the past did not make him smug about the future. He felt there was still important work to be done. He was on his way to New York to coproduce with Oscar Hammerstein II a resplendent new revival of *Show Boat,* for which he had written a new song (his last), "No One But Me," as the concluding number of the production. He also came to discuss a new stage musical about Annie Oakley with the then new producing firm of Rodgers and Hammerstein. That new musical interested him particularly. He had been away from the Broadway stage for almost six years, and it had been over a decade since he had enjoyed success there. He was eager to return to the living theater where he had accumulated so many laurels; to re-establish the imperial position he had once occupied there. Consequently, when friends and physicians advised him against venturing into New York in the difficult winter months he turned a deaf ear. He had not felt better physically in a long time, and his creative energy was at a bursting point.

One little episode, however, seemed ominous and gave him passing concern as he left for New York. In the past he had always permitted himself the luxury of yielding to a superstitious urge to play a few bars of "Ol' Man River" (his good-luck token) before departing on, and immediately after returning from, a trip. En route to the train for New York he suddenly remembered that for the first time he had neglected to perform this ritual.

He arrived in New York on Friday, November 2, 1945, and settled with his wife at the Hotel St. Regis (his daughter, Betty, had remained behind in Beverly Hills). There was an immediate round of social engagements. Many of his friends agreed that it had been years since they had seen him so vigorous, alert, and happy. He had a luncheon date with Guy Bolton and spoke to him about the Broadway musical he was going to do for Rodgers and Hammerstein and which was very much on his mind. "It *has* to be good," Bolton remembers Kern telling him, "in fact it has to be even better than that. Hammerstein has had a number of flops with me, but he has come back to the top of the heap with *Oklahoma!*. Now I *need* a hit of my own to prove myself again."

On Saturday evening, November 3, Kern felt irritable. He had planned to go to a movie, but the milling crowds oppressed him and he went back to his hotel without seeing a show. The following day he went out to the Salem Fields cemetery to visit and place flowers on the graves of his parents, something he never failed to do when in New York. That evening he was a dinner guest in Scarsdale, New York, of his friends the Lee Hartmans, a dinner attended only by the handful of people who had meant most to Kern throughout his life, including Mark Holstein and the Walter Pollaks. To their surprise, Kern—who habitually had been the last to go home from any meeting of friends—decided to leave early, complaining of fatigue. He was gone only a few moments when he suddenly reappeared, saying he had forgotten to say good-bye to Elsie Pollak. "I love you," he told her as he kissed her.

The following morning, after breakfast, Kern told his wife he had some chores to attend to before going over to the Ziegfeld theater at 2 P.M. for the first casting session of *Show Boat*. He wanted to look over some paintings in nearby art shops and to purchase a handsome breakfront as a Christmas gift for Betty. At about noon he was outside the American Bible Society on 57th Street and Park Avenue when he suddenly collapsed. Several passersby rushed to his side. Finding he could neither talk nor move his limbs, they carried him gently inside the Society and placed him on a leather couch. He had lost consciousness. Soon a policeman appeared and identified Kern from his wallet. Despite such identification an ambulance carried him off to Welfare Island and placed him in a public ward with fifty or so patients, some of them derelicts, some alcoholic or mental patients.

That same Monday Eva was having lunch with Dorothy Fields, unaware that at that very hour her husband was stricken nearby. She was not the first to get that news. As it turned out Oscar Hammerstein II was the first. An ASCAP membership card in Kern's wallet led one of the strangers attending him to inform ASCAP which, in turn, reached Hammerstein. Hammerstein rushed out to Welfare Island with his own physician, Dr. Harold Hyman. There Hammerstein tried vainly to arouse some spark of recognition from the unconscious patient, first by talking to him and then by singing "Ol' Man River" to him.

While this was happening, Kern's business manager, William Kron, went out to the Ziegfeld theater to discuss some business with Kern. When he learned there that Kern had been taken to Welfare Island he hurried over to the St. Regis hotel to await Eva's return from her luncheon appointment. It was only then that Eva learned what had happened. A few moments after that, at 2:15 P.M., INS sent a flash to the newsapers: "Police Headquarters said Jerome Kern, 65 [sic], famous composer of song hits, suffered a cerebral hemorrhage and was rushed in serious condition to city hospital."

Because of his critical condition Kern could not be immediately removed from the ward at Welfare Island. All the patients were informed who he was and were entreated, in view of his condition, to maintain utmost quiet. They obeyed out of respect and admiration for Kern; and for the same reason the night nurse voluntarily stayed on duty twenty-four hours to attend him.

"When He Goes Away, Dat's a Rainy Day"   143

Not until Wednesday, November 7, could Kern be transferred to the more congenial setting of Doctors Hospital. There, Hammerstein and his wife, Dorothy Fields, Mark Holstein, and Eva and Betty took rooms to be near Kern around the clock. (Betty, who had been reached with the grim news about her father at 11 A.M. California time by the Beverly Hills police, had immediately come to New York by plane.) Max Dreyfus was one of the few of Kern's most intimate friends unable to be near him; Dreyfus himself was at the time a patient in a Boston clinic.

Kern, who had been placed in an oxygen tent, never recovered consciousness. There seemed to be a slight improvement in his condition for a while, but on Saturday it began to deteriorate alarmingly, and those closest to Kern were warned to expect the worst.

Sunday, November 11, was drab with chill and rain; Eva was suddenly filled with foreboding that Jerry would not survive the day. But only Oscar Hammerstein was in the room when Kern finally succumbed at 1:10 P.M. Hammerstein had steeled himself to expect the inevitable. Yet when Kern's labored breathing stopped and Hammerstein realized Kern was dead, he broke down. Only after he had been able to gain control of himself did he leave the death room to tell Eva, Betty, and the others that Jerry's struggles were over. Soon after that Irving Berlin appeared at the hospital to inquire after Kern's condition; he was the first visitor informed of Kern's passing.

The radio sent word of the death around the country. Before the day ended a touching tribute was presented over the Mutual network with Deems Taylor as master of ceremonies, the first of many to be presented over leading radio stations and networks in the next few weeks. "I know," said Taylor, "my own sorrow at his passing must be shared by the millions who for many years have derived so much pleasure from his lovely tunes."

The funeral ceremony was held in the chapel of Ferncliff Crematory in Hartsdale, New York, on Monday afternoon, at 3 P.M. In respect to Kern's own wishes it was the last word in simplicity. There was no religious service and (except for a blanket of spring blossoms on the coffin) no flowers. Only fifty or so of those who had been nearest and closest to Kern had been invited to attend, among them Hammerstein, Richard Rodgers, Irving Berlin, Edna Ferber, André Kostelanetz, Lily Pons, Cole Porter, Otto Harbach, the Walter Pollaks, Mark Holstein, Howard Reinheimer, William Kron, Deems Taylor, Herbert Fields with his brother Joseph and sister Dorothy, Hassard Short, and Max Gordon. Each was given sprigs of chrysanthemum to place on the coffin before the cremation took place in a simple, nonsectarian ceremony.

Mark Holstein read the twenty-third and thirtieth Psalms. Oscar Hammerstein delivered a brief eulogy.

> We all know in our hearts [he said in conclusion] that these few minutes we devote to him now are small drops in the ocean of our affections. Our real tribute will be paid over many years of remembering, of telling good stories about him, and thinking about him when we are by ourselves. We, in the chapel, will cherish our special knowledge of this world figure. We will remember a jaunty, happy man whose sixty years were crowded with success and fun and love.

The whole country mourned Kern's passing; but it also honored him for the unique place he had so long occupied in American music and the American theater. "Genius is surely not too extravagant a word for him," said the New

York *Herald Tribune* in an editorial, one of many such gestures appearing in American newspapers. "What was this thing he was saying to us in such brave and wistful melody? It is not easy to isolate it, or to appraise its quality with any accuracy. But this we do know: It was something that struck a recognition and a response in the universal heart. . . . He left us rare treasures."

With the co-operation of ASCAP—of which Kern had been a member of the Board of Directors for over two decades—the Columbia Broadcasting System coast-to-coast network presented an hour-long program in memory of Kern on December 9, 1945. Bing Crosby, Nelson Eddy, Dinah Shore, Judy Garland, Hildegarde, Patrice Munsel, and Frank Sinatra were some of the stars of stage, screen, and concert hall to present Kern's greatest songs. Hammerstein read a telegram from President Truman:

> I am among the grateful millions who have played and listened to the music of Jerome Kern, and I wish to be among those of his fellow Americans who pay him tribute today. His melodies will live in our voices and warm our hearts for many years to come, for they are the kind of simple, honest songs that belong to no time or fashion. The man who gave them to us earned a lasting place in his nation's memory.

An impressive program had also been broadcast across the nation on the evening of November 15 by the National Broadcasting Company.

One week after Kern's funeral the distinguished American poet, Joseph Auslander, wrote a tribute which he dispatched to Hammerstein:

> He sang the songs of his lusty land
> In language the people would understand.
>
> . . .

> And now that he will sing no more,
> Our beating hearts will keep the score,
> And in our laughter and our tears
> He will go singing down the years.

And still the honors kept coming. A little over four months after Kern's death—on March 26, 1946—the Hon. Philip J. Philbin of Massachusetts delivered a long eulogy to Kern on the floor of the House of Representatives:

> In the life of our country we have had few such talented and gifted artists as Jerome Kern. Perhaps he marks the end of the most romantic period of music in American history. . . . Americans will continue to sing the beautiful, touching songs, the joyous melodies, the appealing tunes which he wrote, and many of his works will be written in the folklore of American music.

It is fitting to assign the last word of tribute to the man who knew Kern so well, loved him so well, and worked with him so well—Oscar Hammerstein II. "Let us thank whatever God we believe in," he said in the closing lines of his eloquent eulogy at the funeral, "that we shared some part of the good, bright life Jerry led on this earth."

And that we have had the rare privilege of having our lives touched with the enchantment of his music.

APPENDIXES

I. BROADWAY STAGE PRODUCTIONS
(Complete Kern Score or Significant Part of Score)

1911

La Belle Paree. "A jumble of jollity" with book by Edgar Smith, lyrics by Edward Maddern, and additional music by Frank Tours. Presented by the Shuberts at the Winter Garden (opening of the theater) on March 20. Directed by J. C. Huffmann and William J. Wilson. Cast included Al Jolson, Kitty Gordon, and Stella Mayhew (104 performances).

Songs: "That's All Right, Mr. McGilligan"; "Look Me Over, Dearie"; "The Goblin's Glide"; "I'm the Human Brush"; "Paris is the Paradise for Coons"; "Sing Trovatore"; "The Edinboro Glide."

1912

The Red Petticoat. A musical comedy with book by Rida Johnson Young and lyrics by Paul West. Presented by the Shuberts at Daly's theater on November 13. Staged by Joseph W. Herbert. Cast included Helen Lowell, William Pruette, and Grace Field (61 performances).

Songs: "The Waltz Time Girl"; "She's My Girl"; "I Wonder Little Golden Maid"; "The Correspondence School"; "Oh, You Beautiful Spring"; "Where Did the Bird Hear That?"; "Peaches and Cream"; "The Ragtime Restaurant"; "A Prisoner of Love"; "Walk, Walk, Walk"; "Oo-oo-oo"; "Since the Days of Grandmama"; "The Joy of That Kiss."

1913

Oh I Say!. A musical comedy adapted by Sydney Blow and Douglas Hoare from a French play by Keroul and Barré with lyrics by Harry B. Smith. Presented by the Shuberts at the Casino theater on October 30. Staged by J. C. Huffmann. Dances arranged by Julian Al-

148   JEROME KERN

fred. Cast included Joseph W. Herbert, Nellie King, and Alice Yorke (68 performances).

Songs: "How Do You Do?"; "Suzanne"; "A Wife Of Your Own"; "I Know and She Knows"; "Well, This Is Jolly"; "Each Pearl a Thought"; "Alone at Last"; "The Old Clarinet"; "A Woman's Heart"; "Katy-Did"; "I Can't Forget Your Eyes."

1914

The Girl from Utah. A musical comedy with book and lyrics by James F. Tanner, and additional music by Paul Rubens and Sidney Jones. Presented by Charles Frohman at the Knickerbocker theater on August 24. Staged by A. E. Malone. Cast included Julia Sanderson, Joseph Cawthorn, and Donald Brian (120 performances).

Songs: "Some Sort of Girl"; "You Never Can Tell"; "Why Don't They Dance the Polka Anymore?"; "Land of Let's Pretend"; "They Didn't Believe Me" (lyric by Herbert Reynolds); "I'd Like to Wander With Alice in Wonderland" (lyric by James F. Tanner); "We'll Take Care of You All"; "At the Tango Tea."

1915

90 in the Shade. A musical comedy with book and lyrics by Guy Bolton. Presented by Daniel V. Arthur at the Knickerbocker theater on January 15. Staged by Robert Milton. Dances arranged by Julian Alfred. Cast included Richard Carle, Marie Cahill, and William Reynolds (40 performances).

Songs: "Where's the Girl for Me?"; "Jolly Good Fellow"; "I've Been About a Bit"; "Rich Man, Poor Man"; "A Regular Guy"; "Human Nature"; "Whistling Dan"; "A Package of Seeds"; "My Lady's Dress"; "Foolishness"; "Peter Pan"; "The Triangle"; "Wonderful Days"; "My Mindanao Chocolate Soldier."

Nobody Home. A musical comedy with book and lyrics by Guy Bolton and Paul Rubens. Presented by F. Ray Comstock and Elizabeth Marbury at the Princess theater on April 20. Staged by J. H. Benrimo. Dances by David Bennett. Cast included Lawrence Grossmith, Adele Rowland, and Charles Judels (135 performances).

Songs: "Why Take a Sandwich to a Banquet?"; "You Know And I Know"; "Cupid at the Plaza"; "In Arcady"; "The Magic Melody"; "Ten Little Bridesmaids"; "Another Little Girl"; "Bed, Wonderful Bed"; "Any Old Night Is a Wonderful Night"; "The San Francisco Fair."

Cousin Lucy. A musical comedy with book by Charles Klein and lyrics by Schuyler Green. Presented by A. H. Woods at the Cohan theater on August 27. Staged by Robert Milton. Cast included Julian

Eltinge, Dallas Welford, Leo Donnelly, and Olive Tell (43 performances).

Songs: "Those Come Hither Eyes"; "Two Hearts Are Better Than One"; "Society"; "Keep Going."

Miss Information. A musical comedy with book and lyrics by Paul Dickey and Charles W. Goddard. Presented by Charles Dillingham at the Cohan theater on October 5. Staged by Robert Milton. Cast included Elsie Janis, Howard Estabrook, and Melville Ellis (47 performances).

Songs: "Banks of Wye"; "A Little Love But Not for Me"; "Some Sort of Somebody"; "The Mix-Up Rag."

Very Good, Eddie. A musical comedy with book by Philip Bartholomae and Guy Bolton based on Bartholomae's *Over Night*, and lyrics by Schuyler Green. Presented by the Marbury-Comstock Company at the Princess theater on December 23. Cast included Ernest Truex, Alice Dovey, Oscar Shaw, and Ada Lewis (341 performances).

Songs: "We're On Our Way"; "Same Old Game"; "Some Sort of Someone"; "Isn't it Great to be Married?"; "Wedding Bells Are Calling Me"; "On the Shores of Le Lei Wi"; "If I Find a Girl"; "When You Wear a Thirteen Collar"; "Old Neutral Boy"; "Babes in the Wood"; "The Fashion Show"; "I Wish I Had a Million in the Bank"; "Nodding Roses"; "I've Got to Dance"; "Old Bill Baker" (lyric by Ring Lardner).

1917

Have a Heart. A musical comedy with book by Guy Bolton and lyrics by P. G. Wodehouse. Presented by Henry W. Savage at the Liberty theater on January 11. Staged by Edward Royce. Cast included Billy B. Van, Flavia Arcaro, and Louise Dresser (76 performances).

Songs: "Shop"; "I'm So Busy"; "And I'm All Alone"; "I'm Here Little Girl"; "Have a Heart" (lyric by Gene Buck); "Bright Lights"; "The Road that Lies Before"; "Honeymoon Inn"; "Samarkand"; "Come Out of the Kitchen"; "My Wife, My Man"; "You Said Something"; "Napoleon"; "Peter Pan"; "Polly Believed in Preparedness"; "Look in His Eyes"; "Daisy"; "They All Look Alike."

Love o' Mike. A musical comedy with book by Thomas Sidney and lyrics by Harry B. Smith. Presented by Elizabeth Marbury and Lee Shubert at the Shubert theater on January 15. Staged by J. H. Benrimo. Cast included George Hassell, Peggy Wood, Clifton Webb, and Katherine Rogers (192 performances).

Songs: "How Was I to Know?"; "Drift With Me"; "It Wasn't Your Fault"; "Don't Tempt Me"; "We'll See"; "It Can't Be Done"; "Moo Cow"; "I Wonder Why"; "Life's a Dance"; "Who Cares?";

"Hoot Man"; "The Baby Vampire"; "Simple Little Tune"; "It's in the Book."

Oh Boy!. A musical comedy with book by Guy Bolton and lyrics by P. G. Wodehouse. Presented by William Elliott and F. Ray Comstock at the Princess theater on February 20. Staged by Edward Royce. Cast included Tom Powers, Anna Wheaton, Edna May Oliver, and Marion Davies (463 performances).

Songs: "Let's Make a Night Of It"; "An Old-Fashioned Wife"; "You Never Know About Me"; "A Package of Seeds"; "A Pal Like You"; "Till the Clouds Roll By"; "A Little Bit of Ribbon"; "The First Day in May"; "Koo-la-loo"; "Rolled Into One"; "Oh, Daddy Please"; "Nesting Time in Flatbush"; "Words are not Needed"; "Flubby Dub the Cave Man"; "I Never Knew About You"; "Ain't it a Grand and Glorious Feeling?"; "Be a Little Sunbeam"; "Every Day."

Leave It to Jane. A musical comedy with book by Guy Bolton, based on George Ade's play *College Widow*, and lyrics by P. G. Wodehouse. Presented by William Elliott, F. Ray Comstock, and Morris Gest at the Longacre theater on August 28. Staged by Edward Royce. Cast included Edith Hallor, Robert G. Pitkin, Oscar Shaw, and Georgia O'Ramey (167 performances).

Songs: "A Peach of a Life"; "Wait Till Tomorrow"; "Just You Watch My Step"; "Leave It to Jane"; "The Siren's Song"; "There It Is Again"; "Cleopatterer"; "The Crickets Are Calling"; "Sir Galahad"; "The Sun Shines Brighter"; "I'm Going to Find a Girl"; "A Great Big Land"; "What I'm Longing to Say."

Miss 1917. A revue with book by Guy Bolton, lyrics by P. G. Wodehouse, and additional music by Victor Herbert. Presented by Charles Dillingham and Florenz Ziegfeld at the Century theater on November 5. Staged by Ned Wayburn. Cast included Lew Fields, Vivienne Segal, Ann Pennington, and George White (48 performances).

Songs: "Go Little Boat"; "The Land Where the Good Songs Go"; "Tell Me All Your Troubles"; "Cutie"; "We're Crooks"; "I'm the Old Man in the Moon"; "A Picture I Want to See"; "Peaches."

1918

Oh Lady, Lady. A musical comedy with book by Guy Bolton and lyrics by P. G. Wodehouse. Presented by F. Ray Comstock and William Elliott at the Princess theater on February 1. Staged by Robert Milton and Edward Royce. Cast included Carl Randall, Vivienne Segal, Edward Abeles, and Florence Shirley (219 performances).

Songs: "I'm To Be Married Today"; "Not Yet"; "Do It Now"; "Our Little Love Nest"; "Little Ships Come Sailing Home"; "Oh Lady, Lady"; "You Found Me and I Found You"; "Moon Song"; "Waiting Around the Corner"; "The Sun Starts to Shine Again"; "Before I Met

You"; "Greenwich Village"; "A Picture I Had to See"; "It's a Hard, Hard World for a Man."

Toot, Toot. A musical comedy with book by Edgar Allan Woolf, adapted from Rupert Hughes' story, *Excuse Me*, and lyrics by Berton Braley. Presented by Henry W. Savage at the Cohan theater on March 11. Staged by Edgar Allan Woolf and Edward Rose. Cast included Norman Bryan, Rose Kessner, William Kent, and Louise Groody (40 performances).

Songs: "Toot, Toot"; "Quarrel and Part"; "Runaway Colts"; "Kan the Kaiser"; "Every Girl in America"; "A Shower of Rice"; "It's Greek to Me"; "Let's Go"; "The Last Long Mile"; "When You Wake Up Dancing, Girlie"; "Smoke"; "It's Immaterial to Me"; "If You Only Care Enough"; "I Will Knit a Suit of Dreams"; "Honeymoon Land."

Head Over Heels. A musical comedy with book and lyrics by Edgar Allan Woolf suggested by Lee Arthur's dramatization of Nalbro Bartley's story, *Shadows*. Presented by Henry W. Savage at the Cohan theater on April 29. Cast included Mitzi, Lambert Terry, Boyd Marshall, and Joe Keno (100 performances).

Songs: "The Big Show"; "With Type A-Ticking"; "Today Is Spring"; "Any Girl"; "Mitzi's Lullaby"; "Moments of the Dance"; "Me"; "Head Over Heels"; "Vordeveele"; "All the World is Swaying"; "The Charity Bazaar"; "Every Bee Has a Bud of His Own"; "Ladies Have a Care"; "I Was Lonely"; "Funny Little Thing"; "Let Us Build a Little Nest."

Rock-a-bye Baby. A musical comedy with book by Edgar Allan Woolf and Margaret Mayo, and lyrics by Herbert Reynolds. Presented by Selwyn and Company at the Astor theater on May 22. Staged by Edward Royce. Cast included Arthur Lipson, Norah Sprague, Carl Hyson, Frank Morgan, and Louise Dresser (85 performances).

Songs: "Hurry Now"; "Motoring Along the Old Post Road"; "A Kettle Is Singing"; "I Believe All They Said"; "I Never Thought"; "One, Two, Three"; "The Big Spring Drive"; "There's No Better Use for Time than Kissing"; "I Can Trust Myself With a Lot of Girls"; "My Own Light Infantry"; "Little Tune, Go Away"; "Stitching, Stitching"; "Rock-a-bye Baby"; "According to Dr. Holt."

1919

She's a Good Fellow. A musical comedy with book and lyrics by Anne Caldwell. Presented by Charles Dillingham at the Globe theater on May 5. Staged by Fred G. Latham and Edward Royce. Cast included Joseph Santley, Ivy Sawyer, James C. Marlowe, and the Duncan Sisters (120 performances).

Songs: "Some Party"; "The Navy Fox-Trot Man"; "First Rose of Summer"; "A Happy Wedding"; "Jubilo"; "Faith, Hope and Charity";

152   JEROME KERN

"Teacher, Teacher"; "The Bullfrog Patrol"; "Oh, You Beautiful Person"; "Snip, Snip, Snip"; "I Want a Little Gob"; "The Bumble Bee"; "Letter Song"; "Ginger Town"; "Just a Little Line."

1920

Night Boat. A musical comedy with book and lyrics by Anne Caldwell, based on a farce by A. Bisson. Presented by Charles Dillingham at the Liberty theater on February 2. Cast included John E. Hazzard, Ada Lewis, and Louise Groody (148 performances).

Songs: "Some Fine Day"; "Who's Baby Are You?"; "Left All Alone Again Blues"; "Good Night Boat"; "I'd Like a Lighthouse"; "Catskills, Hello"; "Don't You Want to Take Me?"; "I Love the Lassies"; "A Heart for Sale"; "Girls are like a Rainbow"; "Bob White"; "Rip Van Winkle and His Little Men."

Hitchy Koo of 1920. A revue with book and lyrics by Glen MacDonough and Anne Caldwell. Presented by Raymond Hitchcock at the New Amsterdam theater on October 19. Staged by Ned Wayburn. Cast included Julia Sanderson, Florence O'Denishawn, Raymond Hitchcock, Grace Moore, and the Mosconi Brothers (71 performances).

Songs: "Chick, Chick, Chick"; "Millinery Mannequin"; "I Am Daguerre"; "Old Fashioned Dances"; "Sweeties"; "Ding-Dong"; "It's Kissing Time"; "Moon of Love"; "Canajoharie"; "Buggy Riding"; "Old New York"; "We'll Make a Bet"; "I Want to Marry"; "Treasure Island"; "Bring 'Em Back"; "The Star of Hitchy-Koo."

Sally. A musical comedy with book by Guy Bolton; lyrics by Clifford Grey and B. G. De Sylva, and ballet music by Victor Herbert. Presented by Florenz Ziegfeld at the New Amsterdam theater on December 21. Staged by Edward Royce. Cast included Marilyn Miller, Walter Catlett, Leon Errol, and Stanley Ridges (570 performances).

Songs: "On With the Dance"; "Look for the Silver Lining"; "You Can't Keep a Good Girl Down"; "Wild Rose"; "Whip-poor-will"; "Sally"; "The Schnitzka-Komiska"; "The Little Church Around the Corner"; "The Social Game"; "Lorelei."

1921

Good Morning, Dearie. A musical comedy with book and lyrics by Anne Caldwell. Presented by Charles Dillingham at the Globe theater on November 1. Staged by Edward Royce. Cast included Louise Groody, Oscar Shaw, William Kent, Ada Lewis, and Harland Dixon (265 performances).

Songs: "Every Girl"; "Way Down Town"; "Rose Marie"; "Didn't They Believe?"; "The Teddy Toddle"; "Blue Danube Blues"; "Easy

Pickin's"; "Melican Papa"; "Niagara Falls"; "Ka-lu-a"; "Good Morning, Dearie"; "Sing, Song Girl."

1922

The Bunch and Judy. A musical comedy with book by Anne Caldwell and Hugh Ford, and lyrics by Anne Caldwell. Presented by Charles Dillingham at the Globe theater on November 28. Staged by Fred. G. Latham. Cast included Fred and Adele Astaire, Philip Tonge, Johnny Dooley, and Grace Hayes (63 performances).

Songs: "The Naughty Nobleman"; "Pale Venetian Moon"; "Peach Girl"; "Morning Glory"; "Lovely Lassie"; "Every Day in Every Way"; "Times Square"; "Hot Dog"; "How Do You Do, Katinka?"; "Have You Forgotten Me Blues."

1923

Stepping Stones. A musical comedy with book by Anne Caldwell and R. H. Burnside, and lyrics by Anne Caldwell. Presented by Charles Dillingham at the Globe theater on November 6. Staged by R. H. Burnside. Cast included Fred Stone, Allene Stone, Dorothy Stone, Oscar Ragland, and Roy Hoyer (241 performances).

Songs: "Little Angel Cake"; "Because You Love the Singer"; "Everybody Calls Me Little Red Ridinghood"; "Pie"; "Wonderful Dad"; "Babbling Babette"; "In Love With Love"; "Our Lovely Rose"; "Once in a Blue Moon"; "Raggedy Ann"; "Dear Little Peter Pan"; "Stepping Stones."

1924

Sitting Pretty. A musical comedy with book by Guy Bolton and lyrics by P. G. Wodehouse. Presented by F. Ray Comstock and Morris Gest at the Fulton theater on April 8. Cast included Frank McIntyre, Dwight Frye, Queenie Smith, and Rudolph Cameron (62 performances).

Songs: "Is Not This a Lovely Spot?"; "There Isn't One Girl"; "A Year from Today"; "Shuffling Sam"; "The Polka Dot"; "Days Gone By"; "All You Need Is a Girl"; "Dear Old Fashioned Prison of Mine"; "On a Desert Island"; "Enchanted Train"; "Shadow of the Moon"; "Tulip Time in Sing Sing"; "Sitting Pretty."

Dear Sir. A musical comedy with book by Edgar Selwyn and lyrics by Howard Dietz. Presented by Philip Goodman at the Times Square theater on September 23. Cast included Genevieve Tobin, Oscar Shaw, and Walter Catlett (15 performances).

Songs: "Grab a Girl"; "I Want to Be There"; "What's the Use?"; "A Mormon Life"; "Dancing Time"; "To the Fair"; "The Houseboat on the Harlem"; "Seven Days"; "Weeping Willow Tree"; "If You Think It's Love, You're Right."

1925

Sunny. A musical comedy with book and lyrics by Otto Harbach and Oscar Hammerstein II. Presented by Charles Dillingham at the New Amsterdam theater on September 22. Staged by Hassard Short. Dances arranged by Julian Mitchell and David Bennett. Cast included Marilyn Miller, Paul Frawley, Jack Donahue, Mary Hay, Clifton Webb, and Joseph Cawthorn (517 performances).
  Songs: "Sunny"; "Who?"; "So's Your Old Man"; "Let's Say Good Night Till It's Morning"; "D'ye Love Me?"; "The Wedding Knell"; "Two Little Love Birds"; "When We Get Our Divorce"; "Sunshine"; "Strolling, or What Have You?"; "Magnolia in the Woods."

The City Chap. A musical comedy with book by James Montgomery, based on Winchell Smith's *The Fortune Hunter*, and lyrics by Anne Caldwell. Presented by Charles Dillingham at the Liberty theater on October 26. Cast included Richard (Skeets) Gallagher, Phyllis Cleveland, and Irene Dunne (72 performances).
  Songs: "Like the Nymphs of Spring"; "The Go-Getter"; "Journey's End"; "Sympathetic"; "He's the Type"; "The City Chap"; "I'm Head Over Heels in Love"; "Fountain of Youth"; "A Pill a Day"; "Walking Home with Josie"; "Saratoga"; "No One Knows"; "When I Fell in Love"; "Success."

1926

Criss Cross. A musical comedy with book and lyrics by Anne Caldwell and Otto Harbach. Presented by Charles Dillingham at the Globe theater on October 12. Staged by R. H. Burnside. Dances by David Bennett. Cast included Fred Stone, Allene Stone, and Dorothy Stone (206 performances).
  Songs: "Hydrophobia Blues"; "Indignation Meeting"; "Cinderella Girl"; "She's On Her Way"; "Flap-a-Doodle"; "That Little Something"; "In Araby With You"; "Dear Algerian Land"; "Dreaming of Allah"; "Rose of Delight"; "I Love My Little Susie"; "The Ali Baba Babies"; "Bread and Butter"; "You Will, Won't You?"; "Kiss a Four Leaf Clover."

1927

Lucky. A musical comedy with book by Otto Harbach, lyrics by Bert Kalmar, and additional music by Harry Ruby. Presented by Charles Dillingham at the New Amsterdam theater on March 22. Cast included Joseph Santley, Ivy Sawyer, Ruby Keeler, and Mary Eaton (71 performances).
  Songs: "Pearl of Broadway"; "Lucky"; "The Treasure Hunt"; "Without Thinking of You"; "The Pearl of Ceylon."

Show Boat. A musical comedy with book and lyrics by Oscar Hammerstein II, based on the novel of the same name by Edna Ferber. Presented by Florenz Ziegfeld at the Ziegfeld theater on December 27. Dances and ensembles arranged by Sammy Lee. Cast included Helen Morgan, Howard Marsh, Charles Winninger, Edna May Oliver, Jules Bledsoe, and Norma Terris (572 performances).

Songs: "Cotton Blossom"; "Only Make Believe"; "Ol' Man River"; "Can't Help Lovin' That Man"; "Life Upon the Wicked Stage"; "Till Good Luck Comes My Way"; "I Might Fall Back on You"; "C'mon Folk"; "You Are Love"; "Why Do I Love You?"; "In Dahomey"; "Bill" (lyric by P. G. Wodehouse); "Goodbye, My Lady Love"; "Hey, Feller."

1929

Sweet Adeline. A musical romance with book and lyrics by Oscar Hammerstein II. Presented by Arthur Hammerstein at the Hammerstein theater on September 2. Book staged by Reginald Hammerstein. Dances and ensembles staged by Danny Dare. Cast included Helen Morgan, Charles Butterworth, Irene Franklin, and Robert Chisholm (234 performances).

Songs: "Play the Polka Dot"; "'Twas Not So Long Ago"; "My Husband's First Wife" (lyric by Irene Franklin); "Here Am I"; "First Mate Martin"; "Spring Is Here"; "Out of the Blue"; "Naughty Boy"; "Oriental Moon"; "Mollie O'Donahue"; "Why Was I Born?"; "Winter in Central Park"; "The Sun About to Rise"; "Some Girl Is On Your Mind"; "Don't Ever Leave Me"; "Take Me for a Honeymoon Ride."

1931

The Cat and the Fiddle. A musical comedy with book and lyrics by Otto Harbach. Presented by Max Gordon at the Globe theater on October 15. Staged by José Ruben. Cast included Odette Myrtil, George Meader, Georges Metaxa, and Bettina Hall (395 performances).

Songs: "She Didn't Say Yes"; "The Night Was Made for Love"; "Try to Forget"; "One Moment Alone"; "Poor Pierrot"; "A New Love Is Old"; "Ha-cha-cha"; "Don't Ask Me to Sing"; "I Watch the Love Parade."

1932

Music in the Air. A musical comedy with book and lyrics by Oscar Hammerstein II. Presented by Peggy Fears at the Alvin theater on November 8. Staged by Oscar Hammerstein II and Jerome Kern. Cast included Walter Slezak, Katherine Carrington, Tullio Carminati, and Al Shean (342 performances).

Songs: "Melodies of May"; "I've Told Ev'ry Little Star"; "Prayer"; "And Love Was Born"; "I'm Coming Home"; "I Am So Eager"; "One More Dance"; "Night Flies"; "When the Spring is in the Air"; "In Egern on the Tegern See"; "Tingle Tangle"; "I'm Alone"; "The Song Is You."

1933

Roberta. A musical comedy with book and lyrics by Otto Harbach based on Alice Duer Miller's novel, *Gowns by Roberta.* Presented by Max Gordon at the New Amsterdam theater on November 18. Staged by Hassard Short. Dances by John Lonergan. Cast included Tamara, Raymond E. (Ray) Middleton, Bob Hope, Fay Templeton, George Murphy (295 performances).

Songs: "Let's Begin"; "Alpha Beta Pi"; "You're Devastating"; "Yesterdays"; "Something's Got to Happen"; "The Touch of Your Hand"; "I'll Be Hard to Handle"; "Hot Spot"; "Smoke Gets In Your Eyes"; "Ask Me Not to Sing"; "An Armful of Trouble."

1939

Very Warm for May. A musical comedy with book and lyrics by Oscar Hammerstein II. Presented by Max Gordon at the Alvin theater on November 17. Staged by Vincente Minnelli. Dances staged by Albertina Rasch and Harry Losee. Book directed by Oscar Hammerstein II. Cast included Grace McDonald, Jack Whiting, Hiram Sherman, and Donald Brian (59 performances).

Songs: "In Other Words"; "Seventeen"; "All the Things You Are"; "May Tells All"; "Heaven In My Arms"; "That Lucky Fellow"; "L'Histoire de Madame de la Tour"; "That Lucky Lady"; "In the Heart of the Dark"; "The Deer and Park Avenue Lady"; "All in Fun"; "The Lady in Red"; "The Blackbird and the Lady in White."

II. SELECTED BROADWAY PRODUCTIONS WITH INTERPOLATED KERN SONGS

(Note: Name in parentheses is that of the lyricist)

1904

Mr. Wix of Wickham. A musical comedy with book and lyrics by Herbert Darnley and John H. Wagner, and music by Darnley and George Everard. Cast included Frank Labor, Thelma Fair, Harry Corson Clarke, and Julian Eltinge.

Songs: "Angling by a Babbling Brook," "From Saturday 'Til Monday," "Susan," "Waiting for You" (John H. Wagner).

1905

The Catch of the Season. A musical comedy with book by Seymour Hicks and Cosmo Hamilton; lyrics by Charles H. Taylor and others;

and music by Haines, Hamilton, and others. Cast included Edna May.
Songs: "Molly O'Halleran," "Raining" (J. Clifford Harris); "Won't You Kiss Me Once Before I Go?" (C. H. Taylor).

The Earl and the Girl. A musical comedy with book by Seymour Hicks, lyrics by Percy Greenbank, and music by Ivan Caryll. Cast included Eddie Foy and Georgia Caine.
Songs: "How'd You Like to Spoon With Me?" (Edward Laska).

1906

The Little Cherub. A musical comedy with book and lyrics by Owen Hall, and music by Ivan Caryll. Cast included Hattie Williams and Tom Wise.
Songs: "Meet Me at Twilight" (J. Clifford Harris); "A Plain Rustic Ride," "Under the Linden Tree" (M. E. Rourke).

The Rich Mr. Hoggenheimer. A musical comedy with book and lyrics by Harry B. Smith and music by Ludwig Englander. Cast included Sam Bernard and Georgia Caine.
Songs: "Bagpipe Serenade," "Don't Tempt Me," "Don't You Want a Paper, Dearie?" (H. B. Smith); "I've a Little Favor" (M. E. Rourke); "Poker Love" (Paul West).

1907

The Dairymaids. A musical comedy with book by A. M. Thompson and Robert Courtneidge, lyrics by M. E. Rourke, and music by Paul Rubens and Frank A. Jones. Cast included Julia Sanderson.
Songs: "Cheer Up Girls," "I'd Like to Meet Your Father," "The Hay Ride," "I've a Million," "Reasons Why I Love You," "Little Eva," "Mary McGee," "Never Marry a Girl With Cold Feet" (M. E. Rourke).

Fascinating Flora. A musical comedy with book and lyrics by R. H. Burnside and music by Gustave Kerker. Cast included Adele Ritchie, Ada Lewis, and Louis Harrison.
Songs: "Ballooning," "Subway Express" (James O'Dea); "Katie Was a Business Girl" (M. E. Rourke).

Gay White Way. A musical comedy with book by Sydney Rosenfeld and J. Clarence Harvey, and music by Ludwig Englander. Cast included Jefferson de Angelis, Blanche Ring, and Alexander Carr.
Songs: "Without the Girl Inside" (M. E. Rourke).

The Orchid. A musical comedy with book by John T. Tanner and Joseph W. Herbert, lyrics by Adrian Ross and Percy Greenbank, and music by Ivan Caryll and Lionel Monckton. Cast included Eddie Foy and Trixie Friganza.
Songs: "Recipe," "Come Around On Our Veranda" (Paul West).

158   JEROME KERN

1908

Fluffy Ruffles. A musical comedy with book by John J. McNally, lyrics by Wallace Irwin, and music by W. T. Francis and others. Cast included Hattie Williams, Adele Rowland, and John Bunny.

Songs: "Dining Out" (George Grossmith, Jr.); "Meet Her With a Taximeter," "Let Me Carry Your Parasol," "There's Something Rather Odd About Augustus" (C. H. Bovill); "Sweetest Girl, Silly Boy, I Love You" (Wallace Irwin).

The Girls of Gothenburg. A musical comedy with book and lyrics by George Grossmith, Jr. and L. E. Berman, and music by Ivan Caryll and Lionel Monckton. Cast included John E. Hazzard and Louise Dresser.

Songs: "Frieda" (M. E. Rourke); "I Can't Say You're the Only One" (C. H. Bovill).

A Waltz Dream. An operetta with book and lyrics by Joseph W. Herbert, based on a test by Felix Doermann and Leopold Jacobson, and music by Oskar Straus. Cast included Charles Bigelow, Magda Dahl (replaced by Michelina), and Sophie Brandt.

Songs: "Vienna" (Adrian Ross); "I'd Rather Stay Home" (C. H. Bovill).

1909

The Dollar Princess. An operetta with book adapted by George Grossmith, Jr., from a text by A. M. Willner and F. Grünbaum, lyrics by Grossmith, and music by Leo Fall. Cast included Donald Brian, Frank Tinney, and Valli Valli.

Songs: "A Boat Sails on Wednesday" (Adrian Ross and Grossmith); "Not Here, Not Here" (M. E. Rourke).

The Girl and the Wizard. A musical comedy with book by J. Hartley Manners, lyrics by Richard B. Smith and Edward Madden, and music by Julian Edwards. Cast included Sam Bernard and Kitty Gordon.

Songs: "The Blue Lagoon," "Franzi Frankenstein" (Percival Knight).

Kitty Grey. A musical comedy with book and lyrics by J. W. Piggot and music by Lionel Monckton. Cast included Julia Sanderson, Valli Valli, and J. P. Huntley.

Songs: "Eulalie," "If a Girl Wants You," "Just Good Friends" (M. E. Rourke).

1910

King of Cadonia. A musical comedy with book by Frederick Lonsdale, lyrics by Adrian Ross and M. E. Rourke, and music by Sidney Jones. Cast included William Norris, Marguerite Clark, and Mabel Weeks.

Songs: "Catamarang," "Every Girl I Meet" (Percival Knight), "Come Along Pretty Girl," "Lena, Lena," "Mother and Father," "The Blue Bulgarian Band," "Hippopotamus" (M. E. Rourke), "Coo-oo, Coo-oo" (Stonehill).

Our Miss Gibbs. A musical comedy with book and lyrics by James T. Tanner, and music by Ivan Caryll and Lionel Monckton. Cast included Ernest Lambert, Gertrude Vanderbilt, and Bert Leslie.
Songs: "Come Tiny Goldfish to Me" (Hugh Marlowe), "Eight Little Girls" (M. E. Rourke), "I Don't Want You to Be a Sister to Me" (Frederick Day).

1911

Kiss Waltz. An operetta with book by Edgar Smith, lyrics by Matthew Woodward, and music by C. M. Ziehrer. Cast included William Pruette, Robert Warwick, and Adele Rowland.
Songs: "Fan Me With a Movement Slow," "Love Is Like a Little Rubber Band," "Love's Charming Art," "Ta-Ta Little Girl" (Woodward).

Little Miss Fix-it. A musical comedy with book and lyrics by William J. Hurlbut and Harry B. Smith, and music by Nora Bayes and Jack Norworth. Cast included Nora Bayes, Jack Norworth, and William Danforth.
Songs: "There Is a Happy Land," "Turkey Trot" (Norworth).

The Siren. An operetta with book by Leo Stein and A. M. Willner, adapted by Harry B. Smith, lyrics by Harry B. Smith, and music by Leo Fall.
Songs: "Follow Me Around" (Adrian Ross), "In the Valley of Montbijou" (M. E. Rourke), "I Want to Sing in Opera" (David and Arthurs), "My Heart I Cannot Give You" (Matthew Woodward).

1912

The Girl From Montmartre. A musical comedy with book and lyrics by Harry B. Smith and additional music by Henry Bereny. Cast included William Danforth, Richard Carle, and Hattie Williams.
Songs: "Bohemia," "Don't Turn My Picture to the Wall," "Hoop-la," "I'll be Waiting at the Window," "Oo-Oo-Lena" (Robert B. Smith).

Mind the Paint Girl. A play by Sir Arthur Pinero. Cast included Billie Burke, H. E. Herbert, and William Raymond.
Songs: "Mind the Paint" (Pinero), "If You Would Only Love Me" (John Crook).

1913

The Doll Girl. An operetta with book and lyrics by Harry B. Smith, and music by Leo Fall. Cast included Hattie Williams.

160   JEROME KERN

Songs: "If We Were On Our Honeymoon," "A Little Thing Like a Kiss," "Will It All End in Smoke?" (H. B. Smith).

The Marriage Market. An operetta with book by F. Martos, lyrics by Adrian Ross and Arthur Andersen, and music by Victor Jacobi. Cast included Donald Brian.

Songs: "You're Here and I'm Here" (Harry B. Smith), "A Little Bit of Silk," "I'm Looking for an Irish Husband," "I've Got Money in the Bank" (M. E. Rourke).

The Sunshine Girl. A musical comedy with book and lyrics by Paul Rubens and Cecil Raleigh, and music by Paul Rubens. Cast included Julia Sanderson, Vernon Castle, and Joseph Cawthorn.

Songs: "Honeymoon Lane" (M. E. Rourke).

1914

The Laughing Husband. A musical comedy with book and lyrics by Arthur Wimperis, and music by Edmund Eysler. Cast included William Norris, Roy Atwell, and Frances Demarest.

Songs: "Bought and Paid For," "Love Is Like a Violin," "Take a Step With Me," "You're Here and I'm Here" (Harry B. Smith).

When Claudia Smiles. A musical comedy with book and lyrics by Anne Caldwell, and music by Jean Schwartz. Cast included Blanche Ring and Charles Winninger.

Songs: "Sh, You'll Awaken Mr. Doyle" (John Golden).

1915

A Modern Eve. A musical comedy with book by Will Hough, lyrics by Benjamin Hapgood Burt, and music by Victor Hollander and Jean Gilbert. Cast included Leila Hughes, William Norris, and Alexander Clark.

Songs: "I'd Love to Dance Through Life With You," "I've Been Waiting for You" (Harry B. Smith).

1916

Go to It. A musical comedy with book by Anne Caldwell, and lyrics and music by John Golden. Cast included Percival Knight and Gertrude Vanderbilt.

Songs: "When You're In Love You'll Know" (Golden).

Ziegfeld Follies of 1916. A revue with book and lyrics by George V. Hobart and Gene Buck; music by Louis Hirsch, Dave Stamper, and Kern. Cast included Fanny Brice, Ina Claire, Frances White, Bert Williams, and Ann Pennington.

Songs: "Have a Heart," "When Lights Are Low," "My Lady of the

Nile," "Ain't It Funny What a Difference a Few Drinks Make?" (Gene Buck).

1917

Miss Springtime. An operetta with book and lyrics by Guy Bolton, and music by Emmerich Kálmán. Cast included John E. Hazzard and Georgia O'Ramey.

Songs: "When You're Full of Talk," "My Castle in the Air" (P. G. Wodehouse); "Saturday Night" (Herbert Reynolds).

The Riviera Girl. A musical comedy with book by Guy Bolton, lyrics by P. G. Wodehouse, and music by Emmerich Kálmán. Cast included Wilda Bennett and Sam Hardy.

Songs: "Will You Forget?" "Let's Build a Little Bungalow in Quogue" (Wodehouse).

Ziegfeld Follies of 1917. A revue with book and lyrics by George V. Hobart and Gene Buck, and music by Raymond Hubbell and Dave Stamper. Cast included Will Rogers, Eddie Cantor, W. C. Fields, and Fanny Brice.

Songs: "Because You're Just You" (Gene Buck).

1918

The Canary. A musical comedy with book by George Barr and Louis Vereneuil, adapted by Anne Caldwell, with lyrics by P. G. Wodehouse, and music by Ivan Caryll. Cast included Julia Sanderson.

Songs: "Oh, Promise Me You'll Write Him Today" (Edward Clarke); "Take a Chance Little Girl," "Learn to Dance" (Harry B. Smith).

1919

The Lady in Red. A musical comedy with book and lyrics by Anne Caldwell, and music by Richard Winterberg. Cast included Adele Rowland and Donald MacDonald.

Songs: "Where's the Girl for Me?" (Harry B. Smith).

1921

Ziegfeld Follies of 1921. A revue with book, lyrics and music by various writers. Cast included W. C. Fields, Fanny Brice, Raymond Hitchcock, and Van and Schenck.

Songs: "You Must Come Over" (B. G. De Sylva).

1929

Mamba's Daughter. A play by Dorothy and DuBose Heyward. Cast included Ethel Waters, Anne Brown, and Alberta Hunter.

Songs: "Lonesome Walls" (DuBose Heyward).

1930

Ripples. A musical comedy with book and lyrics by Graham John and Irving Caesar, and music by Oscar Levant and Albert Sirmay. Cast included Fred Stone, Dorothy Stone, and Paula Stone.
Songs: "Anything May Happen Any Day" (Graham John).

III. SCORES FOR MOTION PICTURES

1929

Show Boat (Universal), with Laura La Plante, Joseph Schildkraut, and Alma Rubens. This was a part-talking picture with synchronized musical background and songs.

Sally (First National), with Marilyn Miller, Joe E. Brown, and Alexander Gray.
Songs: "Look for the Silver Lining," "Wild Rose," and "Sally."

1930

Sunny (First National), with Marilyn Miller, Lawrence Gray, and O. P. Heggie.
Songs: "Sunny," "Who?", "D'ye Love Me?", "Two Little Blue Birds," "I Was Alone."

1933

The Cat and the Fiddle (M-G-M), with Ramon Navarro, Jeanette MacDonald, Frank Morgan, and Charles Butterworth.
Songs: "She Didn't Say Yes," "The Night Was Made for Love," "Try to Forget," "A New Love Is Old," "Don't Ask Me to Sing," "I Watch the Love Parade," "One Moment Alone," "Poor Pierrot," "Ha, cha, cha."

1934

Music in the Air (Fox), with Gloria Swanson, John Boles, and Al Shean.
Songs: "Music in the Air," "I Am So Eager," "I've Told Ev'ry Little Star," "One More Dance," "The Song Is You," "We Belong Together."

1935

I Dream Too Much (RKO), with Lily Pons, Henry Fonda, and Osgood Perkins. An original score.

Songs: "I Dream Too Much," "Jockey on the Carousel," "I'm the Echo, You're the Song," "I Got Love" (Dorothy Fields).

Reckless (M-G-M), with Jean Harlow, William Powell, and Franchot Tone.
Songs: "Reckless" (Hammerstein).

Roberta (RKO), with Irene Dunne, Fred Astaire, and Ginger Rogers.
Songs: "I'll Be Hard to Handle," "Smoke Gets In Your Eyes," "The Touch of Your Hand," "Yesterdays," "I Won't Dance," "Lovely to Look At."

Sweet Adeline (Warner), with Irene Dunne, Donald Woods, and Hugh Herbert.
Songs: "Don't Ever Leave Me," "Here Am I," "Out of the Blue," "The Sun About to Rise," "'Twas Not So Long Ago," "Why Was I Born?", "We Were So Young," "Lonely Feet."

1936

Show Boat (Universal), with Irene Dunne, Allan Jones, Charles Winninger, Helen Morgan, and Paul Robeson.
Songs: "I Have the Room Above Her," "Ah Still Suits Me," "Only Make Believe," "Ol' Man River," "Can't Help Lovin' That Man," "Gallivatin' Around," "You Are Love," "Bill."

Swing Time (RKO), with Fred Astaire, Ginger Rogers, Victor Moore, and Helen Broderick. An original score.
Songs: "The Way You Look Tonight" (Winner of the Academy Award), "Bojangles of Harlem," "Waltz in Swingtime," "Pick Yourself Up," "A Fine Romance" (Dorothy Fields).

1937

High, Wide and Handsome (Paramount), with Irene Dunne, Randolph Scott, and Dorothy Lamour. An original score.
Songs: "Can I Forget You?", "Alleghany Al," "Folks Who Live on the Hill" (Hammerstein).

When You're in Love (Columbia), with Grace Moore and Cary Grant. An original score.
Songs: "Our Song," "Whistling Boy" (Dorothy Fields).

1938

Joy of Living (RKO), with Irene Dunne and Douglas Fairbanks, Jr. An original score.
Songs: "You Couldn't Be Cuter," "Just Let Me Look at You," "What's Good About Good Night," "A Heavenly Party" (Dorothy Fields).

1940

One Night in the Tropics (Universal), with Abbott and Costello, and Allan Jones. An original score.
Songs: "Back In My Shell," "Remind Me," "You and Your Kiss" (Dorothy Fields).

1941

Lady Be Good (M-G-M), with Eleanor Powell, Ann Sothern, Robert Young, and Lionel Barrymore.
Songs: "The Last Time I Saw Paris," winner of the Academy Award (Hammerstein).

Sunny (RKO), with Anna Neagle, Ray Bolger, and Grace and Paul Hartman.
Songs: "Who?", "Two Little Love Birds," "D'ye Love Me?"

1942

You Were Never Lovelier (Columbia), with Fred Astaire, Rita Hayworth, and Adolph Menjou. An original score.
Songs: "You Were Never Lovelier," "Dearly Beloved," "I'm Old Fashioned," "Wedding in the Spring," "On the Beam" "The Shorty George" (Johnny Mercer).

1944

Can't Help Singing (Universal), with Deanna Durbin, Akim Tamiroff, and David Bruce. An original score.
Songs: "Finale Ultimo," "Elbow Room" "More and More," "Can't Help Singing," "Any Moment Now," "Californi-ay," "Swing Your Sweetheart Round the Fire" (E. Y. Harburg).

Cover Girl (Columbia), with Rita Hayworth, Gene Kelly, and Phil Silvers. An original score.
Songs: "The Show Must Go On," "Who's Complaining," "Put Me to the Test," "Make Way for Tomorrow," "Cover Girl," "Sure Thing," "Long Ago and Far Away" (Ira Gershwin).

Song of Russia (M-G-M), with Robert Taylor and Susan Peters.
Songs: "And Russia Is Her Name" (E. Y. Harburg).

1946

Centennial Summer (20th Century-Fox), with Jeanne Craine, Linda Darnell, Cornel Wilde. An original score.
Songs: "In Love in Vain," "Cinderella Sue," "Two Hearts are Better than One," "Up With the Lark" (Leo Robin), "All Through the Day" (Hammerstein).

Till the Clouds Roll By (M-G-M). The screen biography of Kern with Robert Walker as the composer. An all-star cast included Judy Garland, Van Heflin, Lucille Bremer, Dinah Shore, June Allyson, Tony Martin, Kathryn Grayson, Lena Horne, and Frank Sinatra.
  Songs: "Only Make Believe," "Can't Help Lovin' That Man," "Ol' Man River," "Till the Clouds Roll By," "They Didn't Believe Me," "How'd You Like to Spoon With Me?", "The Last Time I Saw Paris," "I Won't Dance," "Why Was I Born?", "Smoke Gets In Your Eyes," "Who?", "Look for the Silver Lining," "Sunny," "Cleopatterer," "Leave It to Jane," "Go Little Boat," "One More Dance," "Land Where the Good Songs Go," "Yesterdays," "Long Ago and Far Away," "A Fine Romance," "All the Things You Are," the polka from the *Mark Twain* suite.

1949

Look for the Silver Lining (Warner), a screen biography of Marilyn Miller, with June Haver as the Ziegfeld star and a cast including Charles Ruggles and Ray Bolger.
  Songs: "Who?", "Sunny," "Look for the Silver Lining," "Whip-poor-will."

1951

Show Boat (M-G-M), with Kathryn Grayson, Howard Keel, Ava Gardner, and William Warfield.
  Songs: "Why Do I Love You?", "Only Make Believe," "Ol' Man River," "Can't Help Lovin' That Man," "Bill."

1952

Lovely to Look At (M-G-M), an adaptation of *Roberta* with Kathryn Grayson, Red Skelton, Howard Keel, and Ann Miller.
  Songs: "Opening Night," "I'll Be Hard to Handle," "Lafayette," "Yesterdays," "I Won't Dance," "You're Devastating," "Lovely to Look At," "Smoke Gets In Your Eyes," "The Most Exciting Night," "The Touch of Your Hand."

IV. INSTRUMENTAL MUSIC

1902

"At the Casino," for piano. Kern's first published composition.

1940-1941

Transcriptions for string quartet of "All the Things You Are," "The Way You Look Tonight," "Smoke Gets In Your Eyes," "Yesterdays,"

166   JEROME KERN

"Once in a Blue Moon," "The Song Is You," "Bill" (with Charles Miller).

1941

Scenario, for symphony orchestra. World première: Cleveland, Ohio, Cleveland Orchestra, Artur Rodzinski conducting, October 23, 1941.

1942

Mark Twain: A Portrait for Orchestra. World première: Cincinnati, Ohio, Cincinnati Symphony Orchestra, André Kostelanetz conducting, May 14, 1942.

V. KERN'S GREATEST SONGS

"All the Things You Are" (Hammerstein), *Very Warm for May.*
"All Through the Day" (Hammerstein), *Centennial Summer* (introduced by Linda Darnell).
"Babes in the Wood" (Schuyler Green), *Very Good, Eddie.*
"Bill" (Wodehouse), *Show Boat* (introduced by Helen Morgan).
"Can I Forget You?" (Hammerstein), *High, Wide and Handsome* (introduced by Irene Dunne).
"Can't Help Lovin' That Man" (Hammerstein), *Show Boat* (introduced by Helen Morgan).
"Can't Help Singing" (Harburg), *Can't Help Singing* (introduced by Deanna Durbin).
"Dearly Beloved" (Mercer), *You Were Never Lovelier.*
"Don't Ever Leave Me" (Hammerstein), *Sweet Adeline* (introduced by Helen Morgan).
"D'ye Love Me?" (Hammerstein), *Sunny* (introduced by Marilyn Miller).
"A Fine Romance" (Dorothy Fields), *Swing Time* (introduced by Fred Astaire and Ginger Rogers).
"The Folks Who Live on the Hill" (Hammerstein), *High, Wide and Handsome* (introduced by Irene Dunne).
"Here Am I" (Hammerstein), *Sweet Adeline* (introduced by Helen Morgan).
"How'd You Like to Spoon With Me?" (Laska), *The Earl and the Girl* (introduced by Georgia Caine).
"I Dream Too Much" (Dorothy Fields), *I Dream Too Much* (introduced by Lily Pons).
"I'm Old Fashioned" (Mercer), *You Were Never Lovelier.*
"In Egern on the Tegern See" (Hammerstein), *Music in the Air.*
"In Love in Vain" (Leo Robin), *Centennial Summer.*

"I've Told Ev'ry Little Star" (Hammerstein), *Music in the Air* (introduced by Walter Slezak).
"I Watch the Love Parade" (Harbach), *The Cat and the Fiddle*.
"I Won't Dance" (Harbach and Hammerstein), motion picture adaptation of *Roberta* (introduced by Fred Astaire).
"Jockey on the Carousel" (Dorothy Fields), *I Dream Too Much*.
"Just Let Me Look at You" (Dorothy Fields), *Joy of Living*.
"Ka-lu-a" (Anne Caldwell), *Good Morning, Dearie*.
"The Last Time I Saw Paris" (Hammerstein), *Lady Be Good* (introduced by Ann Sothern).
"Leave It to Jane" (Wodehouse), *Leave It to Jane*.
"Look for the Silver Lining" (B. G. De Sylva), *Sally* (introduced by Marilyn Miller).
"Long Ago and Far Away" (Ira Gershwin), *Cover Girl*.
"Lovely to Look At" (Dorothy Fields and Jimmy McHugh), *Lovely to Look At*.
"The Magic Melody" (Bolton), *Nobody Home*.
"More and More" (Harburg), *Can't Help Singing*.
"The Night Was Made for Love" (Harbach), *The Cat and the Fiddle*.
"Nodding Roses" (Lardner), *Very Good, Eddie*.
"An Old-Fashioned Wife" (Wodehouse), *Oh Boy!*.
"Ol' Man River" (Hammerstein), *Show Boat* (introduced by Jules Bledsoe).
"One Moment Alone" (Harbach), *The Cat and the Fiddle*.
"Only Make Believe" (Hammerstein), *Show Boat* (introduced by Howard Marsh and Norma Terris).
"Sally" (Clifford Grey), *Sally*.
"She Didn't Say Yes" (Harbach), *The Cat and the Fiddle*.
"The Siren's Song" (Wodehouse), *Leave It to Jane*.
"Smoke Gets In Your Eyes" (Harbach), *Roberta* (introduced by Tamara).
"The Song Is You" (Hammerstein), *Music in the Air*.
"Sunny" (Hammerstein), *Sunny*.
"They Didn't Believe Me" (Herbert Reynolds), *The Girl from Utah* (introduced by Julia Sanderson).
"Till the Clouds Roll By" (Wodehouse), *Oh Boy!*.
"The Touch of Your Hand" (Harbach), *Roberta*.
"'Twas Not So Long Ago" (Hammerstein), *Sweet Adeline* (introduced by Helen Morgan).
"Waltz in Swing Time" (Dorothy Fields), *Swing Time*.
"The Way You Look Tonight" (Dorothy Fields), *Swing Time* (introduced by Fred Astaire).
"Whip-poor-will" (B. G. De Sylva), *Sally*.
"Who?" (Harbach and Hammerstein), *Sunny* (introduced by Marilyn Miller and Paul Frawley).

168   JEROME KERN

"Why Do I Love You?" (Hammerstein), *Show Boat* (introduced by Howard Marsh and Norma Terris).
"Why Was I Born?" (Hammerstein), *Sweet Adeline* (introduced by Helen Morgan).
"Wild Rose" (Clifford Grey), *Sally.*
"Yesterdays" (Harbach), *Roberta* (introduced by Fay Templeton).
"You Are Love" (Hammerstein), *Show Boat* (introduced by Howard Marsh and Norma Terris).
"You Couldn't Be Cuter" (Dorothy Fields), *Joy of Living.*
"You're Here and I'm Here" (H. B. Smith), *Laughing Husband* (also included in *The Marriage Market*).
"You Were Never Lovelier" (Mercer), *You Were Never Lovelier.*

The following, though never popular and today virtually unknown, deserve inclusion in any list of Kern's most important songs:

"All in Fun" (Hammerstein), *Very Warm for May.*
"Bojangles of Harlem" (Dorothy Fields), *Swing Time.*
"Go Little Boat" (Wodehouse), *Miss 1917.*
"Heaven In My Arms" (Hammerstein), *Very Warm for May.*
"I'd Like to Wander With Alice in Wonderland" (James F. Tanner), *The Girl From Utah.*
"I Never Knew About You" (Wodehouse), *Oh Boy!.*
"In the Heart of the Dark" (Hammerstein), *Very Warm for May.*
"The Land Where Good Songs Go" (Wodehouse), *Miss 1917.*
"Lonesome Walls" (DuBose Heyward), *Mamba's Daughter.*
"Once in a Blue Moon" (Anne Caldwell), *Stepping Stones.*
"Poor Pierrot" (Harbach), *The Cat and the Fiddle.*
"Remind Me" (Dorothy Fields), *One Night in the Tropics.*
"Rolled Into One" (Wodehouse), *Oh Boy!.*
"Seventeen" (Hammerstein), *Very Warm for May.*
"Sure Thing" (Ira Gershwin), *Cover Girl.*
"Two Hearts are Better Than One" (Johnny Mercer), *Centennial Summer.*
"You Know And I Know" (Bolton), *Nobody Home.*
See also "Première Performance" in Appendix VI.

VI. SELECTED RECORDINGS

I. CONCERT WORKS

Mark Twain: A Portrait for Orchestra. André Kostelanetz and his orchestra. Columbia CL-864.

Scenario for Orchestra. Philadelphia Pops Orchestra, André Kostelanetz conducting. Columbia CL-806.

II. MUSICAL COMEDY AND MOTION PICTURE SCORES

Music in the Air. Al Goodman's Orchestra, the Guild Choristers, Jane Pickens, and other vocalists. Victor LK-10025.

Roberta. Al Goodman's Orchestra, the Guild Choristers, Marion Bell, Eve Young, Jimmy Carroll, Ray Charles. Victor LK-1007.

Roberta (Lovely To Look At). Joan Roberts, Jack Cassidy, Kaye Ballard, and other vocalists, with chorus and orchestra conducted by Lehman Engel. Columbia CL-841.

Show Boat. Robert Merrill, Patrice Munsel, Risë Stevens, Janet Pavek, Kevin Scott, Katherine Graves, and chorus and orchestra conducted by Lehman Engel. Victor LM-2008.

Show Boat. (Broadway revival of 1946-1947). Jan Clayton, Charles Fredericks, Carol Bruce, Kenneth Spencer, chorus and orchestra. Columbia OL-4058.

Show Boat. (Soundtrack of the M-G-M motion picture released in 1951). Kathryn Grayson, William Warfield, Howard Keel, and others. M-G-M-3230.

Show Boat. Anne Jeffreys, Howard Keel, Gogi Grant, with chorus and orchestra directed by Henri Rene. Victor LPM 1505.

Show Boat. See *Scenario for Orchestra.* (Concert Works).

Till the Clouds Roll By. (Soundtrack of the M-G-M production of Jerome Kern's life.) Robert Walker, Judy Garland, Dinah Shore, June Allyson, Frank Sinatra, and others. M-G-M-501.

III. SONG COLLECTIONS

The Columbia Album of Jerome Kern. Paul Weston and his orchestra. Columbia 2L-2. "Smoke Gets In Your Eyes," "You Are Love," "She Didn't Say Yes," "They Didn't Believe Me," "Why Was I Born?", "Who?" "Why Do I Love You?", "The Touch of Your Hand," "Look for the Silver Lining," "The Song Is You," "Can I Forget You?", "Just Let Me Look at You," "Lovely to Look At," "In Love in Vain," "I Dream Too Much," "Long Ago and Far Away," "The Folks Who Live On the Hill," "All Through the Day," "The Way You Look Tonight," "Dearly Beloved," "I'm Old Fashioned," "A Fine Romance."

Music of Jerome Kern. Stanley Black and the Kingsway Promenade. London LL-579. "Don't Ever Leave Me," "They Didn't Believe Me," "Who?", "I've Told Ev'ry Little Star," "The Touch of Your Hand," "High, Wide and Handsome," "Ka-lu-a," "In Egern on the Tegern See," "The Way You Look Tonight," "Smoke Gets

In Your Eyes," "The Song Is You," "I Won't Dance," "Look for the Silver Lining."

Music of Jerome Kern. Bing Crosby, Dixie Lee Crosby, and orchestra. Decca A-5001. "Till the Clouds Roll By," "Ol' Man River," "I've Told Ev'ry Little Star," "Dearly Beloved," "All Through the Day," "A Fine Romance," "The Way You Look Tonight."

Music of Jerome Kern. André Kostelanetz and his orchestra. Columbia CL-776. "Smoke Gets In Your Eyes," "I've Told Ev'ry Little Star," "The Song Is You," "Yesterdays," "You Are Love," "Only Make Believe," "Ol' Man River," "She Didn't Say Yes," "All the Things You Are," "They Didn't Believe Me," "The Night Was Made for Love," "Look for the Silver Lining," "Jockey on the Carousel," "The Way You Look Tonight," "I Dream Too Much," "Long Ago and Far Away," "Why Was I Born?", "Why Do I Love You?".

Music of Jerome Kern. Gordon String Quartet. Decca A-5143. "All the Things You Are," "The Way You Look Tonight," "Smoke Gets In Your Eyes," "Yesterdays," "Once in a Blue Moon," "The Song Is You," "Bill."

Première Performance. George Byron sings new and rediscovered Jerome Kern Songs. André Previn as arranger-conductor-pianist. Atlantic 1293. This album includes the following new songs by Kern never before recorded and completely unknown: "Nice to be Near" (Dorothy Fields); "Introduce Me" (Dorothy Fields); "April Fooled Me" (Dorothy Fields). The album also includes: "The Siren's Song," "How'd You Like to Spoon With Me?", "Poor Pierrot," "Two Hearts Together," "The Touch of Your Hand," "Long Ago and Far Away," "Let's Begin," "The Folks Who Live on the Hill," "You Couldn't Be Cuter."

INDEX

Index

Ade, George, 68, 150
"All in Fun," 156, 168
"All the Things You Are," 8, 112, 127, 131, 156, 165, 166, 170
"All Through the Day," 139, 164, 166, 169, 170
"April Fooled Me," 170
Arlen, Harold, 3, 14, 127, 133, 135
Astaire, Fred, 79, 110, 115, 117, 118, 153, 163, 164, 166, 167
"At the Casino" (Kern's first published composition), 3, 30, 34, 165

"Babes in the Wood," 7, 61, 131, 149, 166
Bartholomae, Philip, 60, 149
Berlin, Irving, 3, 73, 77, 79, 114, 121, 122, 133, 143, 144
"Bill," 64, 78, 90-91, 96, 112, 127, 155, 163, 165, 166, 170
"Bojangles of Harlem," 118, 163, 168
Bolton, Guy, ix, x, 4, 18, 43, 54-55, 56, 58, 61-63, 64, 67, 68, 69, 70, 75-76, 78, 87, 137, 140-141, 148, 149, 150, 152, 153, 161, 167, 168
The Bunch and Judy, 79, 152

Caine, Georgia, 38, 41, 157, 166
Caldwell, Ann, 73, 151, 152, 153, 154, 160, 161, 167, 168
"Can I Forget You?", 163, 166, 169
The Canary, 161
"Can't Help Lovin' That Man," 96, 112, 155, 163, 165, 166
Can't Help Singing, 125, 164, 166, 167
"Can't Help Singing," 164, 166
The Cat and the Fiddle, 14, 103, 104, 106, 107, 112, 115, 155, 162, 167, 168
The Catch of the Season, 38, 156-157
Centennial Summer, 139, 164, 166, 168
The City Chap, 154

Comstock, F. Ray, 54, 148, 149, 150, 153
Cousin Lucy, 69, 148-149
Cover Girl, 125, 164, 167, 168
Criss Cross, 86, 154
Cummings, Jack, 74
Cummings, Linda, 74
Cummings, Steve, 19, 74

The Dairymaids, 41, 157
Dear Sir, 153
"Dearly Beloved," 125, 164, 166, 169, 170
De Sylva, B.G., 75, 161, 167
Dillingham, Charles, 80, 83, 149, 150, 151, 152, 153, 154
The Doll Girl, 159-160
The Dollar Princess, 41, 158
"Don't Ever Leave Me," 155, 163, 166, 169
Dreyfus, Max, 7, 35-36, 47, 53, 68, 73, 143
Dunne, Irene, 99, 117, 154, 163, 166
Durbin, Deanna, 125, 164, 166
"D'ye Love Me?", 154, 162, 164, 166

The Earl and the Girl, 37, 38, 157, 166

Fascinating Flora, 157
Ferber, Edna, x, 6, 85-86, 89-90, 144, 154
Fields, Dorothy, 117, 118, 123, 142, 143, 144, 163, 164, 166, 167, 168, 170
"A Fine Romance," 118, 163, 165, 166, 169, 170
Fluffy Ruffles, 158
"The Folks Who Live on the Hill," 163, 166, 169, 170
Freed, Arthur, ix, 136, 139
Friml, Rudolf, 5, 81, 82
Frohman, Charles, 31, 32, 38-39, 53, 148

Gay White Way, 157
Gershwin, George, 2, 3, 7, 14, 71, 80, 113, 123, 127
Gershwin, Ira, ix, x, 18, 62, 125, 127, 133, 135, 136, 164, 167, 168
The Girl and the Wizard, 158
The Girl from Montmartre, 159
The Girl from Utah, 51-52, 53, 112, 121, 148, 167, 168
The Girls of Gothenburg, 158
"Go Little Boat," 150, 165, 168
Go To It, 160
Good Morning, Dearie, 79, 152-153, 167
Gordon, Max, 14, 111, 144, 155, 156
Green, Johnny, 14, 133
Greene, Schuyler, 61, 148, 149, 166
Grey, Clifford, 75, 152, 167, 168

Hammerstein, Oscar II, ix, x, 4, 5, 20, 21, 80, 81, 82, 84, 86-90, 91, 92, 93, 95, 96, 97, 98, 99, 103-105, 106, 107, 110, 113, 114, 123, 126, 137, 140, 141, 142, 143, 144, 145, 146, 154, 155, 156, 163, 164, 166, 167, 168
Harbach, Otto, ix, 4-5, 9, 80-82, 84, 103, 107-109, 116, 144, 154, 155, 156, 167, 168
Harburg, E.Y., 125, 164, 166, 167
Hart, Lorenz, 62, 65
Have a Heart, 63, 69, 149, 160
Hayworth, Rita, 125, 164
Head Over Heels, 69, 151
"Heaven In My Arms," 168
Herbert, Victor, 2, 3, 28, 39, 53, 70, 112, 137, 150, 152
"Here Am I," 107, 163, 166
High, Wide and Handsome, 117, 163, 166
Hirsch, Louis, 65, 70
Hitchy Koo of 1920, 79, 152
Holstein, Mark, 68, 119, 120, 141, 144
Hoschna, Karl, 5, 81

Index

"How'd You Like to Spoon With Me?", 36-37, 38, 45, 138, 157, 165, 166, 170

I Dream Too Much, 116, 117, 162-163, 166, 167
"I Dream Too Much," 163, 166, 169, 170
"I Never Knew About You," 150, 168
"I Watch the Love Parade," 155, 162, 167
"I Won't Dance," 110, 163, 165, 167, 170
"I'd Like to Wander With Alice in Wonderland," 52, 148, 168
"I'm Old Fashioned," 164, 166, 169
"Introduce Me," 170
"In Egern on the Tegern See," 155, 166, 169
"In Love in Vain," 139, 164, 166, 169
"In the Heart of the Dark," 168
"I've Told Ev'ry Little Star," 104, 105, 112, 121, 155, 162, 167, 169, 170

"Jockey on the Carousel," 117, 163, 167, 170
Joy of Living, 117, 163, 167, 168
"Just Let Me Look at You," 163, 167, 169

"Ka-lu-a," 79, 152, 167, 169
Kern, Elizabeth Jane (Mrs. Jack Cummings, Betty), ix, x, 16, 19, 22, 49, 72-74, 120, 123, 140, 141, 143
Kern, Eva (Eva Leale, Mrs. George Byron), ix, x, 19, 43-49, 66-68, 72, 119-120, 123, 124, 134, 136, 137, 140, 142, 143
Kern, Fanny Kakeles, 24, 25, 26, 121
Kern, Henry, 23-24, 25, 26, 29, 121
King of Cadonia, 158-159

Kiss Waltz, 159
Kitty Grey, 158
Kostelanetz, André, ix, 116, 125, 128, 129-130, 144, 166, 168, 169, 170
Kron, William, ix, 68, 119, 120, 142, 144

La Belle Paree, 50, 147
Lady Be Good, 127, 164, 167
The Lady in Red, 161
"The Land Where the Good Songs Go," 150, 165, 168
"The Last Time I Saw Paris," 6, 125-127, 164, 165, 167
The Laughing Husband (See also The Marriage Market), 160, 168
Leave It to Jane, 68-69, 150, 167
"Leave It to Jane," 106, 150, 165, 167
"Let's Begin," 170
The Little Cherub, 157
The Little Thing, 18
"Lonesome Walls," 161, 168
"Long Ago and Far Away," 125, 138, 164, 165, 167, 169, 170
Look for the Silver Lining, 165
"Look for the Silver Lining," 8, 78, 152, 162, 165, 167, 169, 170
Love o'Mike, 3, 69, 149-150
Lovely to Look At, 110, 115-116, 165, 167, 169
"Lovely to Look At," 110, 163, 165, 167, 169
Lucky, 154

"The Magic Melody," 59, 148, 167
Mamba's Daughter, 161, 168
Marbury, Elizabeth, 54, 55, 56, 60, 148, 149
Mark Twain: A Portrait for Orchestra, 23, 129-131, 165, 166, 168
The Marriage Market (See also The Laughing Husband), 160, 168
Men in the Sky, 116
Mercer, Johnny, 125, 164, 166, 168

M-G-M, 17, 136, 139, 162, 163, 164, 165, 169
Miller, Alice Duer, 107, 121, 156
Miller, Marilyn, 76-77, 78, 80, 83, 115, 152, 154, 162, 165, 166, 167
Mind the Paint Girl, 159
Miss Fix-it, 159
Miss Information, 69, 149
Miss 1917, 70, 71, 150, 168
Miss Springtime, 70, 161
A Modern Eve, 160
"More and More," 125, 164, 167
Morgan, Helen, 79, 91, 92, 93, 98, 99, 106-107, 155, 163, 166, 167, 168
Music in the Air, 103-106, 107, 112, 115, 121, 131, 155, 162, 166, 167, 169

"Nice to be Near," 170
Night Boat, 152
"The Night Was Made for Love," 103, 112, 155, 162, 167, 170
90 in the Shade, 55, 148
"No One But Me" (Kern's last song), 98, 140
Nobody Home, 56, 59-60, 148, 167, 168
"Nodding Roses," 7, 61, 149, 167

Oh Boy!, 63, 64, 112, 150, 167, 168
Oh I Say!, 51, 147-148
Oh Lady, Lady, 64, 78, 91, 150-151
"An Old-Fashioned Wife," 150, 167
"Ol' Man River," 8, 89-90, 96, 101, 112, 121, 131, 140, 142, 155, 163, 165, 167, 170
"Once in a Blue Moon," 127, 131, 153, 166, 168, 170
"One Moment Alone," 103, 155, 162, 167
One Night in the Tropics, 117, 164, 168
"Only Make Believe," 96, 101, 155, 163, 165, 167, 170
The Orchid, 157

Our Miss Gibbs, 159

Pollak, Elsie, ix, 68, 119, 120, 141, 144
Pollak, Walter, ix, x, 37, 68, 105, 141, 144
"Poor Pierrot," 103, 155, 162, 168, 170
Porter, Cole, 3, 7, 133, 144
Princess Theatre Shows, 6, 56, 58-59, 60, 62-63, 64-65, 68, 75, 91, 102

Reckless, 163
The Red Petticoat, 51, 147
Reinheimer, Howard, ix, 17, 144
"Remind Me," 164, 168
Reynolds, Herbert, 151, 161, 167
The Rich Mr. Hoggenheimer, 41, 157
Ripples, 162
The Riviera Girl, 161
Roberta, 107-110, 112, 115, 156, 163, 167, 168, 169
Rock-a-bye Baby, 69, 71, 151
Rodgers, Richard, ix, 2-3, 4, 7, 65, 97, 98, 99, 114, 140, 141, 144
Rogers, Ginger, 110, 115, 117, 118, 163, 166
"Rolled Into One," 168

Sadler, Frank, 59
Sally, 75-77, 78, 79, 91, 106, 112, 115, 152, 162, 167, 168
"Sally," 152, 162, 167
Sanderson, Julia, 41, 52, 79, 121, 148, 152, 157, 158, 160, 161, 167
Savage, Henry W., 63, 69, 70, 149, 151
Scenario for Orchestra, 100-101, 128, 130, 131, 166, 169
Schwartz, Arthur, 3, 4, 8, 133
"Seventeen," 156, 168
"She Didn't Say Yes," 103, 155, 162, 167, 169, 170
She's a Good Fellow, 151-152

Index

Show Boat, 6, 51, 64, 78, 85-87, 88-90, 91-96, 97-101, 102, 105, 106, 107, 112, 115, 128, 131, 137, 139, 141, 154-155, 162, 163, 165, 166, 167, 168, 169
The Shuberts, 51, 57, 77, 147, 149
The Siren, 159
"The Siren's Song," 69, 131, 150, 167, 170
Sitting Pretty, 80, 153
Slezak, Walter, 103, 121, 155, 167
"Smoke Gets In Your Eyes," 8, 9, 109, 110, 112, 127, 131, 156, 163, 165, 167, 169
"The Song Is You," 104, 112, 127, 155, 162, 166, 167, 169, 170
Song of Russia, 125, 164
Stamper, Dave, 70, 160, 161
Stepping Stones, 79, 131, 153, 168
Stone, Allene, 73, 79, 86, 153, 154
Stone, Dorothy, 72, 79-80, 86, 153, 154, 162
Stone, Fred, 73, 79, 86, 153, 154, 162
Sunny, 80, 82, 83-84, 87, 106, 112, 115, 154, 162, 164, 166, 167
"Sunny," 154, 162, 165, 167
The Sunshine Girl, 160
"Sure Thing," 164, 168
Sweet Adeline, 106, 107, 115, 155, 163, 166, 167, 168
Swing Time, 117, 118, 163, 166, 167, 168

"They Didn't Believe Me," 2, 7, 52-53, 112, 121, 131, 148, 165, 167, 169, 170
Till the Clouds Roll By, 53, 137-138, 165, 169
"Till the Clouds Roll By," 64, 112, 121, 150, 165, 167, 170
Toot, Toot, 69, 151
"The Touch of Your Hand," 110, 156, 163, 165, 167, 169, 170
" 'Twas Not So Long Ago," 107, 155, 163, 167

"Two Hearts are Better Than One," 139, 149, 164, 168
"Two Hearts Together," 170

Very Good, Eddie, 2, 60-62, 63, 112, 149, 166, 167
Very Warm for May, 110-112, 131, 156, 166, 168

A Waltz Dream, 41, 158
"Waltz in Swing Time," 163, 167
"The Way You Look Tonight," 8, 118, 127, 163, 165, 167, 169, 170
Weston, Paul, 9, 10, 169
When Claudia Smiles, 160
When You're in Love, 117, 163
"Whip-poor-will," 78, 152, 165, 167
"Who?", 83-84, 112, 131, 154, 162, 164, 165, 167, 169
"Why Do I Love You?", 90, 96, 101, 155, 165, 168, 169
"Why Was I Born?", 107, 112, 155, 163, 165, 169, 170
"Wild Rose," 78, 152, 162, 167
A Winsome Widow, 50
Mr. Wix of Wickham, 6, 34, 40, 156
Wodehouse, P.G., ix, x, 4, 32-33, 61-63, 64, 67, 68, 69, 70, 76, 78, 91, 149, 150, 153, 155, 161, 166, 167, 168
Wolff, Maurice, ix, 27, 28
Woollcott, Alexander, 12, 73, 86, 119, 120-121
The Woman Haters, 41

"Yesterdays," 110, 112, 127, 156, 163, 165, 168, 170
"You Are Love," 96, 155, 163, 168, 169, 170
"You Couldn't Be Cuter," 163, 168, 170
"You Know and I Know," 59, 148, 168
You Were Never Lovelier, 125, 164, 166, 168

"You Were Never Lovelier," 164, 168
Youmans, Vincent, 3, 80, 82
Young, Rida Johnson, 51, 147
"You're Devastating," 156, 165
"You're Here and I'm Here," 2, 7, 160, 168

Ziegfeld, Florenz, 50, 51, 57, 70, 75-76, 77, 78, 80, 86, 87-89, 92-93, 98, 150, 152, 155
Ziegfeld Follies of 1916, 70, 160-161
Ziegfeld Follies of 1917, 161
Ziegfeld Follies of 1921, 161

WITHDRAWN
No longer the property of the
Boston Public Library.
Sale of this material benefits the Library.

glittering era: *Sally, Roberta, Music in the Air,* and, of course, *Show Boat*—the American classic that is perhaps Kern's greatest monument.

Interlaced throughout the book are warm glimpses of a successful man who enjoyed living and lived well: his youth in New York City and on the Continent, his marriage to Eva Leale, his days as friend and host to the famous of Broadway and Hollywood.

Copiously illustrated with nostalgic photographs, THE WORLD OF JEROME KERN includes listings of Kern's songs, as well as the Broadway productions and motion pictures for which he wrote the scores.

About the author

With THE WORLD OF JEROME KERN, David Ewen adds another triumph to his brilliant musical biographies, among them *A Journey to Greatness: The Life and Music of George Gershwin,* and *Richard Rodgers.* Called "music's interpreter to the American public," Mr. Ewen is also the author of the *Complete Book of the American Musical Theater,* numerous biographies for young people, and many standard reference works in the field of serious music. He has been a frequent contributor to the music sections of leading magazines and newspapers.

HENRY HOLT AND COMPANY, INC.
383 Madison Avenue, New York 17
Chicago   PRINTED IN U.S.A.   San Francisco